Adrenaline

My Untold Stories

ZLATAN IBRAHIMOVIĆ

with Luigi Garlando

Translated by Antony Shugaar

PENGUIN BOOKS

PENGUIN BOOKS

UK | USA | Canada | Ireland | Australia
India | New Zealand | South Africa

Penguin Books is part of the Penguin Random House group of companies
whose addresses can be found at global.penguinrandomhouse.com.

Penguin
Random House
UK

Translated from the Italian *Adrenalina – My Untold Stories*
First published in Italy by Cairo 2021
First published in Great Britain by Penguin Books 2022

001

Copyright © Zlatan Ibrahimović, 2021
© RCS MediaGroup S.p.A., Milan, 2021
English-language translation copyright © Word Row Inc., 2022

The moral right of the copyright holders has been asserted

Set in 12.5/14.75pt Garamond MT Std
Typeset by Jouve (UK), Milton Keynes
Printed and bound in Great Britain by Clays Ltd, Elcograf S.p.A.

The authorized representative in the EEA is Penguin Random House Ireland,
Morrison Chambers, 32 Nassau Street, Dublin D02 YH68

A CIP catalogue record for this book is available from the British Library

ISBN: 978-0-241-99608-9

www.greenpenguin.co.uk

*I love bicycle kicks. I love kicking the ball high in
the air, using my feet, even though they're
the lowest part of my body.*

*Before dropping back to earth, there's that moment
when I see everything upside down, and that's when
everybody else – my teammates, the referee, the fans – is
suddenly turned on their heads. It's an exclusive, privileged
view of the world. Mine and mine alone.*

*So let me dedicate this book to everyone who likes
to overturn the usual rules and expectations. Because it's
only by following your instincts, with tenacity and
determination, dedication and grit, that your
own vision of the world can be unique like mine.*

Contents

Pre-game (*Adrenaline and Balance*)   1

1 The Bicycle Kick (*or About Change*)   7

2 Dribbling (*or About Freedom*)   41

3 The Opponent (*or About War*)   66

4 The Ball (*or About Love*)   83

5 The Agent (*or About Wealth*)   103

6 The Journalist (*or About Communication*)   134

7 The Goal (*or About Happiness*)   147

8 The Referee (*or About the Law*)   167

9 The Injury (*or About Pain*)   187

10 Passing (*or About Friendship*)   208

Extra Time (*or About the Future*)   233

Index   241

Pre-game
(*Adrenaline and Balance*)

Okay, I give up.

I'm forty years old.

I'm a god, but I'm also a god who's getting old.

I'm finally coming to terms with it, just like I'm coming to terms with the fact that my body isn't what it used to be. For years I've ignored the signals my body's been trying to send me, but at last I've decided to pay attention. I can't dart back and forth and sprint the way I did when I was young; if I get tired or I get clattered, it takes me longer to recover. I've modified my style of play to match this new body of mine. I no longer spend the whole match in the penalty area where shots fly in all directions. I don't necessarily shout for the ball any more; instead I create play for the team. These days I'm more likely to be assisting other players' goals than trying to score them myself. I'm no longer looking for the spotlight – I've won everything I needed to win. Now it's more about inspiring my young teammates and helping them to grow and mature.

I'm forty and I have two sons who are no longer boys; they're already young men. Generally speaking, at this age you draw a line under everything you've done and you start working on a reckoning – a first rough review of what your life has been and meant.

That's what this book is about.

For days and days I've been trying to pretend nothing is happening, ignoring the fact that my birthday is drawing closer. I've tried to keep from seeing the number forty, but then last night there it was, enormous and bright red, covering the entire façade of a hotel. They'd created it by lighting up some rooms and leaving others dark.

In that Milan hotel, my wife Helena threw a surprise party that touched me deeply. My nearest and dearest were there, friends from all over the globe, the most important people in my life. There were legends of the football world, trainers and coaches, even players I've treated badly on the pitch. I didn't expect to see all those people in one place, on that terrace.

Gennaro 'Rino' Gattuso, who had been head coach at Napoli, explained it to me this way: 'You've always been your authentic self, even when you were beating them up. That's why they showed up.'

Helena did a great job. She organized the whole thing while managing to keep it a secret. She gave me a wonderful gift. Usually it's me who presents gifts to others.

I've already told many times the story of how I left my neighbourhood to become a world football champion. I grew up with a battered Select soccer ball glued to my foot, dribbling my way around anyone who put themselves in my path in the Rose Garden – Rosengård, the name of my childhood neighbourhood – which was home to immigrants of all kinds. The slightest spark was enough to start us banging heads. But that tiny patch of hard-packed dirt was the workshop where I built my game, the school where I learned the tricks that made me Ibra.

I was born to a couple who divorced early. I shuttled back and forth between a mother who worked herself to death to put food on our table and a father whose refrigerator was often empty. What I lacked, I went and got for myself. I would steal bikes and clothing because I was sick of being made fun of at school. I always wore football socks instead of normal ones, and Malmö team tracksuits that I stole from the dressing room.

Then football yanked me out of the ghetto and guided me towards a very different way of life. I landed in Amsterdam, where I bought my first Porsche and met Mino Raiola, my agent. He and my wife Helena are, and always will be, the two most important people in my life.

Mino is much more than an agent and businessman to me. He's a friend, a brother, a father – everything, really. He charted the route my career would follow, mapped my triumphs, helped me get out of my toughest moments and solved thousands of problems for me. The more pain and suffering I was going through after some injury, the closer to him I felt. From the Netherlands, Mino took me to Italy, then Spain, France, England and America, then back to Italy.

Helena has always been more mature and responsible than I am. She's helped me to stop and think, she's taught me common sense and good taste. She knows how to recognize and create beautiful things – she has a distinct gift for elegance. That was her vocation, and it will continue to be even after I stop playing. Over the years she's plucked the sharper thorns out of my somewhat wild personality and, most important of all, has given me the gift that's precious above anything else: my sons.

But if everyone is familiar with Ibra the football player, they still don't know Ibra the man.

I'm now going to try to tell you about me, at this midway point, as my story as a football player is coming to an end and a very different future approaches – a future that, for now, waits to be clearly defined.

Each chapter of this book starts out with stories from the pitch and concludes with reflections on everyday life: from goals to happiness, from referees to justice, from assists to friendship, from injuries to death . . .

I don't hang back, I don't play-act, I don't pretend – it's just like Gattuso told me. I'll admit, for instance, that the thought of quitting makes me deeply anxious. The closer I come to the day I leave football, the greater my fear for the future: where will I find the adrenaline that in my present life I get from facing defenders like Giorgio Chiellini?

'Adrenaline', the title of this book, is a key word in my life.

In everything I do I need to perceive a challenge and then devote to it all the passionate defiance that I possess. I need to give it my heart. That's how it's always been, and that's how it always will be for me. I need to feel the adrenaline pumping in my veins.

Now, at the age of forty, with two grown sons, that adrenaline pumps differently, because these days I have different needs. Whereas I used to be aggressive with referees, now I help them. I used to love throwing down a challenge and carrying the banner of just one side, but now I'll go to Sanremo and feel deeply moved at the outpouring of love and respect I feel from my Italian fans. It's also true, though, that when I feel too many people pressing in on me, I have trouble breathing. That's when I go down to my garage, rev up one of my prize possessions, pull onto the motorway, jam my foot down on the accelerator – and *vroom*, I'm gone. Or I'll go for a walk in the woods in search of freedom. I seek out other people, but I also flee from them.

It's not the only contradiction in my personality, and I'm well aware of that. I've always been a bundle of contradictions – they're simply part of me. The new thing is that I'm doing my best to keep them under control, just as I've learned to master my more impulsive reactions. It's rare for defenders to succeed in getting me to rise to the bait, the way they so often did at the start of my career. I no longer give in to instinct. I think I've become more balanced. Credit for that goes to the passage of time and to Helena and Mino. I seek out balance in everything I do. And that goes for the way I've raised my boys: I make up for the strong discipline by showering them with plenty of love.

I used to be pure adrenaline, but now I'm *adrenaline* and *balance*.

This book isn't the gospel of a god. It's the diary of a forty-year-old man coming to terms with his past and looking the future right in the eyes, as if it were yet another adversary for me to take on.

1. The Bicycle Kick
(or *About Change*)

It's evening and we've just come home from dinner out at a restaurant. My mobile phone rings.

Helena makes a wild guess: 'Mino?'

She's right: it's my agent, Mino Raiola. But it hadn't been a difficult guess. He'd been calling repeatedly for days. After the time I spent with Los Angeles Galaxy, and after our elimination from the MLS Cup Play-offs, I'd decided to hang up my boots, and Mino was doing everything in his power to change my mind.

He was giving it one more try now. 'Zlatan, someone playing at your level and with your history can't simply retire while he's in America. People will say you're a coward, that you've gone soft, that you settled for the easy way out. What's become of the lion of football, the King of the Forest?'

'I'm done, Mino. I'm not playing any more. Face it.'

But he persists. 'No. You need to come back to Europe and prove to everyone that you can still compete against the best, in spite of your injury in Manchester. Even if only for six months, from January to June. Face up to this challenge and then you can do whatever you want. You're

7

Ibra. So you need to leave the stage as Ibra. I can get you another contract whenever I like.'

'Listen, Mino, there's only one way you can convince me: with adrenaline. I don't need any old contract – I need a challenge that'll pump adrenaline into my veins. Do you have that?'

At the age of thirty-eight I could still give it my all in gruelling training, put up with the pain and keep going, but in the morning when I got out of bed I needed to be able to answer that question: why are you doing it, Zlatan?

And the answer had to be: because all this pain and suffering will ultimately come back to me in the form of adrenaline and make me feel great.

A few evenings later I was at home watching the HBO documentary about Diego Armando Maradona. At one point it shows footage of an old Napoli match and focuses on the crowd at the San Paolo stadium. The place is full. The director concentrates on the kop, young men packed tight, singing, shouting, pounding drums. There's an incredible crackling electricity.

I sit up on the couch and pay close attention, and I start to feel the adrenaline pumping in my veins – right there in the veins on my neck. *Thump, thump, thump* . . . I phone Mino right away: 'Call Napoli. I'm going to SSC Napoli.'

'Napoli?'

'Yes, I'm going to play for Napoli.'

'Wait, are you sure about this?'

'You want me to go on playing? My adrenaline will come

from Napoli's fans. I'll fill the stadium with eighty thousand people every match I play, and I'll make that team win the Scudetto,* just the same as it did back in Diego's day. Winning the Italian championship will drive the whole town crazy. That's where my adrenaline will come from.'

So we reach out to SSC Napoli, we talk terms and we come to an agreement. It's all settled. I'm a Napoli player.

The coach is Carlo Ancelotti and I know him well; we worked together in Paris. He's overjoyed to work with me again, and we talk practically every day. He explains how he intends to play me.

I haven't talked to the club president, Aurelio De Laurentiis, but I already know him. I met him a few years earlier when I was on holiday in Los Angeles with my family. De Laurentiis had heard I was staying in the same hotel as him, and he left a note for us at the reception desk: 'This evening you're invited to this restaurant.' There was a card with the address. It seemed more like an order than an invitation. 'Let's go,' I said to Helena immediately. We spent a very enjoyable evening together.

I identify a house in Posillipo – an affluent part of Naples – that might be good for me, seeing as I'd only have to stay for six months. Everyone tells me that the city's pretty chaotic. I'm even considering if I might want to live on a boat.

The day I'm supposed to sign, 11 December 2019, De

---

* The decorative shield in the colours of the Italian flag, which is displayed on the shirts of the Italian sports clubs that won the championship of their respective sport in the previous season.

Laurentiis fires Ancelotti. Right in the middle of the season . . . I get a bad feeling inside when I hear about it. Damn, that's not a good sign. Maybe I can't trust this club president. A guy like that can't guarantee stability for me and my teammates. Plus, I know that, even if Rino Gattuso – the new manager – is a friend, he needs another kind of centre forward for his 4-3-3 formation. In fact he never even got in touch.

Everything's off.

A few days later I call up Mino and I ask him, 'Who needs me most? Which team is in the deepest shit?' I'm not looking for a contract. I am looking for a challenge.

'AC Milan just lost to Bergamo, 5–0.'

Theoretically the last thing I'd want to do is go back to a team I'd previously played for, because of the risk I might do worse the second time around. But this time is different. Milan had lost 5–0.

I tell Mino, 'Call Milan. Let's go to Milan.'

My challenge would be to take one of the most prestigious clubs on Earth back to the top. If I'm able to do that, it'll be worth more than anything I've done with all the other teams.

That's my adrenaline.

At first we talked to Paolo Maldini, the technical director, and – truth be told – it didn't go well.

Sure, I admit I'm the one who chose to come to Milan, I offered myself; but if you want me on your team, you need to give me determination and excitement, you need to show me trust: you have to convince me. You can't just keep telling me that I'm thirty-eight. I know how to keep track of my own birthdays.

Paolo wasn't reassuring me, any more than the president of Napoli had. Then Zvonimir Boban – at that time Milan's chief football officer – became part of the conversation and we started talking turkey. Zvone was far more confident and he told me, 'Zlatan, ask for whatever you want and I'll give it to you.'

There, that's the way you talk to Ibra.

So Ibra comes back to AC Milan.

I didn't know Stefano Pioli well, but that was not a problem. For me the relationship with coaches has never been that important; I've always had a very professional relationship with them. The only problems I ever had were with Pep Guardiola, but they were *his* problems with *me*, not mine with him, and I never even knew exactly what those problems were. They were his problems.

I studied my new teammates and immediately decided: these guys have no idea what it means to play for Milan.

The AC Milan I used to know was made up of players like Gattuso, Andrea Pirlo, Massimo Ambrosini, Alessandro Nesta, Cafu and Thiago Silva . . . The old guard. If you were doing less than your best in training, you'd get a shoulder to the face. They didn't talk much, but they'd still make it clear you were out of line.

Now, however, I could see that nearly everyone was moving slowly at training sessions. I couldn't just stand by and watch. I'd come to Milan to change things, to start a revolution.

I'm not going to name names, but I asked one player, 'Hey, excuse me, why aren't you running?'

And he replied, 'You're wrong, I *am* running.'

I wouldn't take that for an answer. 'No, that isn't running. Are you waiting around and hoping someone else will run for you? You know when I'll be willing to run for you? When you help me win something. But in your whole life you've never won a fucking thing. Now start playing and *start running*.'

And he started running.

My teammates listened to me with a mixture of respect and fear. I carefully studied their reactions: if someone collapses after you criticize them, they aren't going to make it; if they get back on their feet and make changes, then they are. Those were the players I needed.

What we all had to learn was how to suffer, how to fight every second of the match, fight for every centimetre of pitch. We had to become a strong, tight group, like one single entity, because that was the only way we could hope to win.

We were no longer the AC Milan that I'd known ten years ago. If all we had was quality, we weren't going to win anything, because there were other teams much stronger than we were. We couldn't hang around dribbling and twiddling our thumbs; we couldn't bide our time, waiting for the perfect moment to let one player make a solo move. We had to win each match by fighting for ninety minutes straight. But that's an attitude you can only learn through practice, by giving your all every single day.

If I saw someone wasn't pulling their weight, I'd tell

them so, loud and clear and to their face, even before Pioli got a chance to do so. And I wouldn't do it off to one side, where no one else could hear. I'd do it in front of the team, because what I had to say to one member of the team went for all the others who were standing around listening.

In training I'm always the tough guy – I bust everybody's balls.

But after working like that, day after day, there was a growing team spirit, a greater willingness to make sacrifices, as well as a stronger bond between me and the rest of the players, and a deeper sense of my responsibility towards my teammates. Every time I walked into the dressing room I could sense that my fellow players were watching me, as if to ask, 'So, Ibra, what are we doing today?' It was a sensation that pumped me up. It was the challenge I'd been looking for.

As a result, we did better and better on the field.

But then, after Boban left, things span out of control and you couldn't tell what was happening. It was impossible to decipher the present, far less the future for AC Milan. We players, Pioli and his staff – we all felt like a single body, united and determined, but it was the body of a 'dead man walking', a Death Row convict heading for the electric chair.

If a new coach was coming, we'd all be sacked, and rumour had it that Ralf Rangnick was on his way; it would not only be Pioli who was sacked, but me too, as well as Maldini and Frederic Massara, the technical director and the sporting director respectively. All of us. We agreed:

the only way to respond to this situation was to produce results every day. Talking back or grumbling among ourselves wouldn't do any good. We had to work hard, sweat and suffer, and make progress: that was the only answer. We believed in what we were doing. And that's how we'd become even stronger.

But then one day I decided there was too much gossiping, too many rumours swirling around, and it was time to get some clarity.

It was June 2020. Maybe not the ideal moment for it, because the next day we were going to have to play the match of our lives, the Coppa Italia semi-final against Juventus, but Chief Executive Officer Ivan Gazidis was in Milanello – the Milan training centre – and I decided to take advantage of the opportunity.

In front of the whole team I told him, 'Ivan, no disrespect, but we need to make a few things clear. In just one month, lots of contracts are going to expire. What are we all supposed to do? Extend the leases on our apartments? No one knows. What about the team for next year? No one knows. There's no sense of security. What are we fighting on behalf of? The team deserves respect and clear answers.'

He told us that Rangnick wasn't coming, he reiterated his commitment to Pioli and we talked about lots of things.

Gazidis wasn't used to serving as CEO the way it's done in Italy, where it means working in close contact with the team. Personally it was breaking my heart, because I remembered the AC Milan I'd known ten years earlier – a club with a strong identity. Now things were completely different.

I didn't want everything to go back to the way it had once been. I knew that was impossible. I'm a professional and I adjust to the situation as I find it, but I did expect a minimum level of dialogue in any case.

Sure enough, after that day things improved, because when there's something eating at you deep inside, it's always best to get it out into the open.

Ivan got closer to the team. Paolo started talking more with me and the other players. At first he was still largely a footballer and, to a much smaller degree, a director. If you change profession, you have to forget what you were before. The team needs to respect you as a director, not for what you did as a footballer. And Paolo had grown, both in terms of attitude and experience.

The Milanello revolution was a success.

In training, I was seeing an incredible hunger. If we lost, the team was furious. By now we all had the right attitude. Everyone was finally figuring out the proper way to be AC Milan footballers. And I didn't let up even a little, being determined to set the proper example.

There were days when my body was a wreck, and Pioli started to notice. During training he'd tell me, 'Zlatan, you don't have to make this run.'

And I'd reply, 'Coach, if I run, every one of them will run, and they'll listen to what I have to say. Otherwise it all just becomes hot air.'

In fact everyone was saying to themselves: 'Hell, if Ibra is willing to run, then we have to run, too, because that's how he won everything he's won. So we have to work the way he has.'

The only player I couldn't figure out how to wake up was Rafael Leão. I tried everything I could think of, but I never found the key. I was kind, I was tough, I was indifferent. I managed to make it work with everyone else, but I couldn't do it with him. In the end I came to the conclusion that, if someone doesn't wake up on their own, there's really not much you can do.

But I did manage to wake up Hakan Çalhanoğlu. I would say to him, 'Hakan, do you realize what it means to wear the number ten for Milan, with the history that it carries? Do you know who wore that shirt before you? You need to achieve major things, and so far you haven't done a thing.'

I pushed him and pushed him and, in the end, he rose to the occasion. When you're playing with really outstanding teammates like Hakan, it all becomes so much easier.

Plenty of the guys matured and grew – in terms of personality as well. Take Gigio Donnarumma, for instance. When I met him, he practically never opened his mouth. I forced him to shout on the pitch. 'Gigio, don't tell me how young you are. I couldn't care less. You're here because you're strong and you have skills. You need to help the team achieve its mission.'

I couldn't be the only one talking out on the pitch. I wanted to develop other leaders.

When the ultras (somewhere between a fanatical fan and a hooligan, in English) came to Milanello to protest against Donnarumma for dragging his feet on his contract renewal, I told the directors, 'Let me go out and talk to them. Here we share collective goals – we're not in it for ourselves. The fans can have their say at the end of the season, but right now we're battling to make it into the Champions League. Let me explain it to them. I'll just ask them, "Do you want to be able to watch the Champions League next year, yes or no? If you do, leave us alone and let us play. You can come round after it's all over and engage in theatrics and do whatever else you want. But how can you protest against Gigio now? We need Gigio. Without him, what do you think we're going to achieve?"'

But they refused to let me go out and talk to them.

We grew and we matured, and we fought a great season. The fact that Inter Milan had a good shot at winning the Scudetto was something everyone was saying that summer. But the idea that AC Milan would come in second? Nobody was predicting that. What *we* did was far more spectacular and impressive than what Inter did. Of course if we'd gone on to win, that would have been an entirely different matter. But from the very first day of the 2020–21 season I was absolutely positive we were going to win the Scudetto, because this was our time.

Pioli was really good at bringing out the best in the players we had on our team. With his organizational skills and our vibrant new spirit, we spent a long time in first place. When our team began to flag as a collective, the quality of the individual players ought to have made up for the general decline and kept us going, but we didn't have the raw material that other teams could field, and it hurt us.

One day in the dressing room I decided to ask, 'Raise your hand if you've ever played a match in the Champions League.'

The only ones who raised their hands were Ciprian Tătăruşanu and Çalhanoğlu. I was shocked.

When Inter made five substitutions, they'd bring on equal or stronger players, whereas we'd field equal or weaker ones. In fact I suggested to the club, 'We need to fight to limit the number of substitutions to just three, otherwise Inter and Juve will benefit.'

All the same, in spite of the fact that we had a weaker squad, and despite the many injuries, we held up our heads and staved them all off. No one believed in us. We alone were convinced we could do it. And we finished second.

Before the decisive match against Atalanta, the last game of the season, I told the guys, 'Do you remember when I asked how many of you had ever played before in the Champions League? Now you have a match awaiting you that can change the answer you give. Do you want to play in the next Champions League? Let them see it out there, on the pitch.' And then as we left the dressing room, before the match started, I announced to everyone, 'We're going to win today.'

I was sure of it. I didn't have to wait for the match. I'd already seen all I needed to see in the eyes of my team-mates, and I'd already realized all I needed to know from the tension in the dressing room.

They played a perfect match, full of team spirit, a sense of sacrifice and a willingness to suffer. They never once gave away the ball, and they didn't surrender an inch of pitch. We were Milan – the real Milan – a team with heart, a team that had trained for months in Milanello.

And to think that we were playing against Atalanta, the same team that had inflicted five goals on Pioli when I was still in LA, in search of a challenge that would pump adrenaline into my veins.

I found it and I won it, but not only in terms of results on the pitch. In all my time playing football I've never had such a strong bond with my teammates. I've never felt so beloved in a dressing room.

So I turned around AC Milan. I've always had a weakness for turnarounds, reversals, upsets.

And the finest of them all? Well, come on, there's no comparison . . .

First and foremost because we were playing against the English, who had always had so many bad things to say about me. Things like: 'Ibra's never scored a goal against England'; 'Ibra's never scored a goal against an English team'; 'Ibra has always avoided the Premier League'; 'Ibra acts like a diva'; and so on and so forth, blah-blah-blah. They'd had me in their sights ever since I played in the Netherlands, and they didn't stop when I went to Italy and then France.

All right then. It was time to play this match against them.

It was 14 November 2012 and it was the first match played in the Friends Arena, the new stadium in Solna, a suburb of Stockholm. It was only an international friendly, Sweden vs England, but it meant a lot more than that to me. I had a score to settle with the English.

When they snipe at me constantly, it charges my batteries. I've always used criticism like petrol poured on the flames. It makes me work harder to prove what I've got.

Ever since I was a boy I was always the centre of attention, for better or worse. It was partly my fault – no doubt about it – because I was a talker. I'd tell anyone who'd listen that I was the best, or that sort of thing, because I felt so confident. So whenever I got something wrong or did something bad, I presented twice the target. And it simply made me feel even stronger.

That night the English fans sang, 'You're just a fake Andy Carroll.' The only way he resembled me was in his height.

The match begins and the stadium is packed: 60,000 spectators. And it's immediately a battle royal.

They want to prove something, and we can't come off looking bad, here at home, especially not when we're playing the first match in our new stadium. I'm wearing the number ten on my back and the captain's armband on my arm. After twenty minutes we're leading 1–0 – a low cross, I head for the ball, there's a scuffle, the ball stays right there, I kick it with the tip of my toe: goal!

'That's good,' I say to myself. 'I just scored the first goal in this new stadium. That will go down in history.'

England strikes back and then overtakes us: 2–1.

I run to meet the ball, stop it with my chest, then I kick: 2–2. But in that play Gary Cahill gets hurt, so I'm in no mood to celebrate; plus, all we've done is even the score. I don't celebrate a draw. Like in Bergamo on the last day of the season, when Milan won and qualified for the

Champions League. Everyone was celebrating out on the pitch, and I was very happy, no doubt about it, and contented, but I wasn't celebrating. I don't celebrate a second-place finish. I never have and I never will: I only celebrate coming first.

England gives away a free kick. I kick it hard, sending the ball skimming along just off the ground, and I nail it right into the corner of the net. Now we're in the lead: 3–2. There, I've scored a hat-trick in our new stadium.

What else are the English going to have to say now? That it was merely a friendly, blah-blah-blah?

It's close to the end of the game. The fans are streaming out of the stadium because the parking facilities haven't yet been completed and it's hard to get your car in and out. Then this long ball comes sailing in, kicked by our defence, more to run down the clock than anything else. I want to intercept it, as always.

Instinct told me to do it: go! Then, while I'm running, I'll figure out whether or not I'm in time.

I spot the goalie Joe Hart running out of the box. What's he doing? Cahill stops short so that he doesn't collide with him. So now I decide: I need to do something to make sure the ball winds up where I want it to go, and not where *he* wants it to go. I have two choices: either I opt for a tackle with the goalie or I pretend to do so, but then pull back at the last second.

Hart sees that I'm coming towards him, but when he shifts his glance to the ball, I pull back. He heads it badly, and the ball goes straight up in the air and drops towards me.

I'm oblivious to what's going on around me – whether anyone from the opposing team is heading towards me, or anything else. I remain completely focused on the ball and, with my back to the net, think only about positioning my shoulders in the direction of the goal, because I'm so confident that if I connect with the ball it'll wind up in the net.

I kick the ball from thirty metres out and, while it's still in the air, I turn to look.

Usually, when doing a bicycle kick, I put my hands out right away to protect myself, and I take care to land safely. Not this time: it doesn't matter if I break something. The only thing I care about at this point is watching how the kick unfolds, because Ryan Shawcross is running towards the goalposts and he might intercept the ball. No, please, don't let that happen . . .

Shawcross throws himself at it in a sliding skid, but he can't make it in time and the ball hits the net.

So I take off my shirt and start running, bare-chested, crazed with joy. I've attained the most I could ever hope to achieve in a match.

Against England!

Sure, you guys keep on talking about me. This is my answer. I throw my shirt in the air, I see the Swedes going nuts and the English players looking at me strangely.

I walk past Danny Welbeck and tell him, 'Enjoy, because you'll never see anything like this again.'

I've got goosebumps at this point. From the way people are looking at me, I realize I've done something that isn't normal. And when it dawns on you that you've achieved something that will go down in history, there's a very special feeling that fills you up, right in your chest – something that will never leave you.

There's a little bit of everything in that goal: courage, imagination, acrobatics, strength, risk and arrogance. Just about everything.

I *am* that bicycle kick. It's my finest calling card, my signature move.

A normal player would have let the ball hit the ground and then tried to score, from thirty metres out.

If I'd fluffed the bicycle kick, they would have said: 'That's Ibra for you, the big show-off . . . He doesn't have a brain. Why does he do it?' But I still would have tried it again at the next opportunity I got, because when I challenge what is possible, it makes me feel stronger and more confident. Once you've been up there – once you've touched the summit of the possible and you've proved you can do it – you want to get back there at every chance you have.

When it comes to bicycle kicks, my love of martial arts (and especially Taekwondo) plays a role. It's given me agility, acrobatic skills and flexibility. It's taught me movements that aren't common in football: kicking or stopping the ball six feet in the air, or striking it with a back-heel.

Every time medical staff check my knee, they assume it's broken and that the cruciate ligament has been stretched out of shape. Actually it's just really elastic, because of all the training I do. I even have flexible bones.

I've worked out and exercised ever since I was a child.

My father would put on Bruce Lee and Jackie Chan videos. They were his idols, and he'd play those tapes for me and my sister. Then when I walked down the street, I'd try to kick everything within reach: lamp posts, rubbish bins – I'd knock over everything I could.

I was crazy about kicking things, so instinctively I would rely primarily on my feet during my childhood games of football. I always tried to use my feet, where other people might use their head. That's one reason why, even now, I'm not exactly at the top of the rankings when it comes to headers, although you'd certainly expect that of a striker who's six feet five inches tall. For me, footwork has always mattered much more on the pitch than heading. I tried to score my goals with bicycle kicks rather than headers: first, because it was more spectacular, but also because I felt much more confident doing it.

Plus, putting your head where your feet normally go, every now and then, helps: it gives you a different outlook.

On life as well as on football.

Pelé's bicycle kick in the film *Escape to Victory* is something everyone remembers.

I met Pelé at an awards ceremony in Sweden. He gave me the prize for best player in the country. A deep honour and a thrill.

Legends like Pelé and Maradona are what makes you want to start playing football in the first place. You don't start by watching a football match; you start by watching legends like them on television – legends like Johan Cruyff and Zinedine Zidane, players who make you want to see what you can do, who fill you with the joy of the game.

I don't know them personally, but Maradona struck me as more authentic: he did everything from the heart; he was never afraid to talk, to run risks; he had no filter, he didn't care about presenting a perfect self-image. When he made a mistake, it was a mistake from the heart. That's why he touched you more than anyone else.

Nowadays 95 per cent of all footballers have a filter around them and seem obsessed with projecting a perfect image. I don't even know what that's about. As far as I'm concerned, you can only be yourself, and you're only perfect if you manage this. Make mistakes, learn from your mistakes. In time you'll make more mistakes. But you'll remain yourself.

But these players have an entourage of people around them, protecting them, shielding them, to create this perfect image, and so people think: 'Oh, this is a wonderful person.' But it's not necessarily true; they're just hidden behind a filter. Maradona never gave a thought to his image, but he followed his instincts. If a 'Hand of God' can bring me a trophy, then I'd be happy to score that goal. But I much prefer my goal against England. That goal taught the English a real lesson.

I also scored a goal like that – well, more or less like that – when I was playing for Ajax, against Breda. It all happened in a flash, it was so fast.

I was past one opposing player, then a second and a third ... With every touch, my strength, my conviction and my adrenaline increased. I was extremely focused, but

I could hear the crowd shouting. With each touch, they'd shout: 'Shoot! Shoot! Shoot!' And each time I told myself: 'No! No! No!'

And then when the ball finally sailed into the net, the feeling of joy was overwhelming – not so much because I'd scored the goal, but because I'd shown them that I was right. The best moment to shoot is when *Ibra* decides to shoot.

I tried to make a difference with football. To distinguish myself. If I'd wanted to get involved in politics, I would have been a politician. But I didn't do that: I became an athlete. An athlete unites people, a politician divides them. It's been my good luck, thanks to sport, to get to know other guys from all over the world. We live in the same dressing room, and we fight as one. If it hadn't been for football, I would never have met them and I'd know nothing about their cultures. Are you a Muslim? Are you a Catholic? It doesn't matter. All that matters is basic respect in the dressing room.

When my statue was unveiled in Malmö, I said, 'Kids, tomorrow you have my permission to stay home from school. Come and see me, and say hello . . .'

A few critics took it a little too seriously, but then they understood it was just a playful joke and, more importantly, was done for a good cause: as a way of being close to the young people of my city. I have a special bond with children and young people, and an understanding that I have a harder time establishing with grown-ups. Youngsters fill me with an incredible surge of energy. I feel a natural chemistry that I can't explain and that has nothing to do with what I might, or might not, say.

I understand that even a smidgen of attention can be very important to them, so I always try to set aside time for young people, because they're the future and because I remember that, when I was their age, I never had this opportunity to meet famous people who could give me advice, inspiration and energy. I did everything on my own.

It was me, in my little world, against *them*, in their great big world.

My statue in Malmö was taken down.

The Swedish Football Association and I had unveiled it in October 2019. A month later the news got out that I'd purchased shares in Hammarby, a football club in Stockholm where my sons now play. It was the owners of the Los Angeles Galaxy who'd suggested I make the investment, while we were negotiating my contract renewal. They had a certain number of shares, and I bought 25 per cent. It seemed like a good opportunity to do something useful for Sweden. To me, it was an act of gratitude to my country.

But the Malmö ultras really took it the wrong way. Not so much the investment itself, but mostly something I said: 'I'll turn Hammarby into the strongest club in Scandinavia.' But what else was I supposed to say? In all the adventures into which I've ever plunged, I've always tried to give my best.

I know it would have been better to invest in my home town, but the opportunity presented itself in Stockholm, and that's where I had chosen to live. And that's when people started defacing the statue of me that stood outside the stadium: they broke off its nose, they sawed off a foot, they hung toilet seats over its arms, they wrapped a noose around its neck and they even tried to set it on fire.

The city of Malmö put up a fence to protect the statue, but it wasn't enough. In January 2020 vandals managed to topple it, by cutting the legs out from underneath it. I have to assume it was young kids. The generations that knew me well would never have done that, because they know that I did something good for Malmö, and for Sweden.

I was especially sorry for Peter Linde, the sculptor who made the statue. It really is a nice statue: it's me with my arms thrown wide. I remember seeing it flat on the ground, its head wrapped in a black T-shirt.

In some odd way, that statue is a metaphor for my life: everywhere I've gone, people have tried to put me on a pedestal, and then they have tried to knock me off it. It happens to lots of successful people.

That wasn't an easy period. I was worried about my relatives who live in Stockholm. Among other things, threatening graffiti started to appear on the city walls. They called me a Judas.

There was lots of talk about where to place the statue. Definitely not near the stadium. I don't even know where they're keeping it now.

But I do know that I'm standing on my own two feet, at the age of forty.

*

Marco van Basten is another player who performed insane bicycle kicks. Everyone remembers the ones he scored against FC Den Bosch for Ajax, and against Göteborg for Milan. Ajax and Milan – just like me. I developed as a player with that comparison dangling like a sword over my head.

When I was at Ajax, Marco was assistant coach to Ronald Koeman and he told me in secret, 'Don't pay any attention to the coach, Zlatan. Save your energy and use it all on attack.'

The reason he said it was that he remembered the way Arrigo Sacchi had hammered him when they were at AC Milan: 'Go back and do it again, help your team, work even without the ball, press the opposing team, participate in play . . .'

The same things they'd told me to do at Ajax.

Sacchi was a revolutionary. He turned football upside down – that's clear to me. But he always had it in for me, and I never quite understood the reason why. I've been told that he even recommended that Guardiola did not sign me for Barcelona.

Two great friends. Friends to each other, I mean. Not friends to me.

Sacchi had a column in the Italian sports paper *Gazzetta dello Sport* and it seemed to me that he criticized me more on personal terms than professionally. Now that's something I can't accept. If I hate a teammate, I behave impeccably towards him out on the pitch, treating him the same as everyone else. And I expect the same level of professional behaviour from those who write, and from those who critique for a living. If you have something to criticize me about personally, then say it to me; don't tell the world, because it's not your job to judge me personally. You're paid to judge me professionally.

So one day when I met Sacchi on live TV after a Champions League match, in a television studio, I told him loud and clear what I thought about it, right to his face. Because I can hold things in for a year, two years, five years, but I don't forget. Like with Marco Materazzi, for instance — more on that later.

The words van Basten said to me filled me with pride. When someone of that stature tells you something like that, you have to think: 'He's a living legend, I'm playing in the same position, everyone compares me to him, so I'm going to listen to *him*, not the coach.'

During matches Marco's advice always came to mind, and I'd tell myself: 'Hold on, Zlatan, don't go over there; stay right here and save your strength for a good attack.' Because back then the football I was playing was pure rock 'n' roll and I worked extra-hard to prove I could do anything I set out to do. I thought more about myself than about how I could best help the team.

In that sense van Basten changed me, but my real transformation came under the tutelage of Fabio Capello. He definitely turned me around, because with him it wasn't lip service; it was relentless work and repetition. Every day he'd say to me, 'I need to strip away all the Ajax you have in your body and pound into your mind one idea: the goal, nothing but the goal.' And: 'The best way to help your team is to score goals. You remind me a lot of van

Basten, but you still don't know how to move inside the penalty area the way he does, to get to the net.'

Every day Capello would send me out, line me up with the ball in front of goal and have me take fifty shots: bam, bam, bam! The great Italo Galbiati, assistant to the coach, was constantly behind me, practically sinking his fangs into the back of my neck. When I got things wrong, he'd poke at me. 'You see? You just don't have the stuff for this . . .' That would only pump me up even more: *bam*, goal!

And he'd say, 'Still not good enough.'

Bam, goal! 'Was that good enough for you?' I'd ask him.

Bam, goal! 'How about that one? Was that good enough for you?'

Bam, goal!

He always took my adrenaline to the extreme. We got along like a house on fire. Every day like that, for six to eight months. And when he was done with me, I'd turned into a goal machine.

I walked onto the pitch with a different kind of radar.

At Ajax I used to say, 'Give me the ball and I'll show you something spectacular.' At Juve, 'Give me the ball and I'll score a goal.' I'd changed. I'd become a different person.

Of course Wayne Rooney's bicycle kick in the Manchester derby will go down in history. Beautiful play. Wayne is a great person. Only when I played alongside him did I come to realize how powerfully he burns inside for football, and quite how much work he puts in for his team in any given match.

Rooney played eighteen seasons in the Premier League, which amounts to far more than a lifetime, because there is no league more gruelling than the English one: the pace is faster, the play is more aggressive; there are more matches, and there was no winter break until recently. Eighteen seasons like that.

I watched him. I was four years older than Rooney and I was the one who should have felt worn out, yet I seemed much younger. And in fact, in the end, Rooney could no longer do what José Mourinho asked, and he didn't play much in my Manchester United.

We met back up in the MLS in the US.

I went there to turn things around.

I said to myself: 'All right, I'll go there and teach them what football really is, because they don't seem to know.'

I found myself in a different world – far too limited – where time passes slowly and the day they dream of, when 'soccer' explodes into the country's consciousness, never seems to arrive. Where what seems to enjoy the greatest success and popularity is women's football. What's lacking are, primarily, the knowledge, the foundation, the fundamentals.

At Galaxy there were guys who'd just arrived from academies or from college teams, who didn't know how to move on the pitch. I would take them aside and tell them, 'Listen, that's no way to defend. You can't simply stand there in front of me like a fence post; you need to come at me at an angle, so that you force me to move left or right.'

But things like that – say, basics like posture – are things that a young person can't expect to learn in the first team, they've got to have learned them before that. By the time they make it to the first team, they have to be ready to play hard and win. Recruiting top-flight players such as Henry, Pirlo and Ibrahimović doesn't help you to grow. Having those figures is useful in terms of showmanship, and to offer a benchmark in terms of what you aspire to – the highest level you can reach for – but the most useful things are training, coaches and the basic knowledge that helps to establish a foundation. You can't base a strategy on recruiting eleven Zlatan Ibrahimovićs and hope that'll be the simple solution.

Plus, it went entirely against my idea of how things work. I saw teammates who would lose a match, go back into the dressing room and start laughing it off. I blame the play-offs. It was the top seven teams that qualified for the finals, so winning those matches in the first part of the season almost didn't matter. But ever since the day I was born I've always wanted to win, even during training. It's eat or be eaten: I want to be the one doing the eating.

One day I explained it to the journalists: 'The play-off system is disgusting.' They collectively fainted, the way they did when I told them, 'I'm a Ferrari surrounded by Fiat 500s', because football in America is nothing but a play-off.

I'd come to America to make my mark. But my team-mates looked at me in one of two ways. Either: 'Wow . . .' Or: 'This guy's only here to pick up a fat pay cheque and get out of here as quick as he can.' But that's not the way it was.

So one day I explained it very clearly in the dressing room. 'Listen up, guys. I didn't come to Los Angeles to spend time on the beach or take a sightseeing tour of Hollywood. Anyway I don't care about your American dollars. I'm here because I have a mission to accomplish. You need me, and I need you to accomplish that mission. If you think otherwise, let me know immediately and I can go home. I'm not here for a holiday.'

They'd answer me, 'Don't worry, Zlatan, we're getting into play-off mood now.'

What the hell is 'play-off mood' supposed to be? That's not the way it works.

We have to be winners all year round, not for two weeks a year. 'Then why don't we draw up new contracts?' I asked, provoking them where it hurt most. 'We could just skip our pay cheques for the first part of the season, because we're not giving it a hundred per cent anyway. We could start demanding pay cheques only after the play-offs start. Sound okay, guys?'

I give 100 per cent from the first session, on the first day of training, because training is when you start winning. There's not a single match that I don't consider part of the finals, because every match has a winner and a loser, and I want to be the winner, every time. That's what I wanted to teach the Americans; that's how I wanted to help them grow. For a while they were lucky enough to learn, up close and personal, how real top-flight football works.

Then I left and said, 'So long; now you can go back to playing baseball.'

I turned France around after a defeat at Bordeaux. The referee failed to penalize a back-pass to the goalie. How could he do that? It's against the rules. The referee tells me, 'I made a wrong call earlier and, with this mistake, we're even.'

What kind of excuse is that? I'm losing the match and you tell me, 'I got that one wrong and now I get this one wrong, too.'

But I did understand that it's not easy being a referee. When the big signings all arrived, Paris Saint-Germain was transformed within twenty-four hours into a team of superstars. Our immense popularity, on the pitch and off, took us to another dimension. The referees, who don't even do this job full-time, needed to grow and get used to this new level of play, but we had no time to wait for them to catch up. We were being paid a lot, there was plenty of pressure and we were expected to win.

The French judged me every time they looked at me.

And so, with my adrenaline pumping because of the referee's mistakes and the unjust defeat by Girondins de Bordeaux, I thundered, 'France, you piece-of-shit country, you don't deserve me and you don't deserve PSG.' We were something spectacular, and it seemed France didn't want anything spectacular within its borders. We were just too much, and they considered us a mistake.

After letting off that barrage, I went out into the street and took a look around. I told myself: 'Watch out, Zlatan, be ready to react in case anything happens.' But out of ten people, ten told me, 'You're right, it's a piece-of-shit country.'

Well, that's strange . . . Let's see what the next person has to say.

'You're absolutely right, Ibra.'

I never expected that reaction from the French people.

Right from the beginning of my whole story I'd vowed one thing over all others: whatever happens to me – success, wealth, fame – I won't change. I have to remain myself, because if I change, I'll disappoint myself. If I came up from the street, I have to remain exactly who I was, the same person, even if I make it to the top.

In France I followed that same philosophy: I'm not going to change, and if I have something to say, I'll say it. That's why they thought I was arrogant. The French have a hard time accepting any forms of behaviour that are different from theirs. They don't know how to say, 'I'm like this, he's like that – we're just different.' No, instead anyone who veers away from their models of behaviour is criticized and considered wrong.

The ones who really took it the wrong way were the ex-players, because I would say that I was the best footballer ever to set foot in France, and that kind of thing. But I didn't say it because I was arrogant; I said it because I believe in myself, because I was convinced of it.

In 2014 I won a prize as the finest footballer in France and I had to do a radio interview with Frank Leboeuf, a one-time defender on the French national team. Live. I liked that, because that way I could be sure people would listen to everything I had to say. They wouldn't be able to cut out or modify a recording. I've said it before: when I keep something inside, I can wait for as long as ten years, but I don't forget. And when the time comes, I bring it up.

And that time had arrived for Leboeuf.

We started talking and he said to me, 'But, seriously, Ibra, your attitude . . .'

Here we go.

I stopped him and said, 'Yeah, right, my attitude. Let me tell you something, Frank. I find it to be a very strange thing, this issue of my attitude you always seem to want to talk about. According to you, I'm arrogant, but around the world the people who are really notorious for their arrogance are the French. So it must mean that I'm one of you. So really, you ought to be proud of me, because I represent your arrogance in the best of all possible ways.'

Leboeuf stopped talking. I'd knocked him dead.

People wanted to expel me from France after the insults I'd unleashed in Bordeaux. Marine Le Pen said more than once that I needed to leave the country. Even the Swedish ambassador got involved. The matter shifted onto political territory, and I didn't like that one bit. After all, my insults were bound up with a football match, so I thought they should judge me as an athlete, not attack me on a personal level. If I wanted to cause controversy, I could have pointed out that I paid more taxes than any French citizen. I was giving something to the country – there was no denying that. Still, all I said was, 'Enough, let's put an end to this bickering.'

But the controversy actually served my purposes, in a

certain sense. When the time came round to renew my contract with PSG, I said, 'All right, if you'll replace the Eiffel Tower with a statue of me, I might consider extending.'

Whereupon they lost it. I mean, they were really pissed off. I loved their reaction, because if I provoke them and they react, it means that I've won.

Like the time I posted an X-ray on Instagram of a hand with a middle finger extended. Everyone else uses social media to build up their number of followers, but what I wanted was reactions.

If people react, that means I win.

I don't know whether love or hatred has turned me around more in my life. I do know one thing, though: when someone hates you, you know they hate you; when someone loves you, you can never tell if it's true love.

When I played for Inter, the fans loved me. When I left, what became of that love?

When I'm out on the pitch, feeling that I'm loved really gives me a stunning surge of energy. But then hatred pumps me up, too. When they piss me off, they take me to a higher level: I'm more careful, I'm stronger, I have a greater desire to prove something. If they hate me, they make me better. And that's why football matches like derbies charge me up the way they do. They fill me with energy and a special kind of anger that elevates me. Nowadays, though, I have much greater self-control than I used to when I was younger.

That's partly because having children has brought me a

tranquillity and a balance that I used not to have. Until my firstborn arrived, I would bring football home and, with it, all of my rage. Then things changed. I'd come home, take one look at my kids and forget everything else. They turned my life around. They came into my life and suddenly football stopped being the most important thing. All that mattered was that my sons were all right.

I made an effort to make sure they were raised by Zlatan, not Ibra. I did everything within my power to erase the footballer and make sure that all they saw was the father, because when they were small, my kids hated football. They could see that their papa belonged to everyone and was more the property of the fans than theirs: television cameras, photographers, autographs, the stadium – it was all just one big Ibra.

If I took them out to a field to kick a football around, one son would cry and the other would bird-watch. Then one day they started playing *FIFA* on their PlayStation and they discovered Neymar, Lionel Messi, Gianluigi Buffon, Francesco Totti . . . They came to me and said, 'Papa, there are other champions out there.'

Of course there are lots of them – it's not as if Ibrahimović is the only one.

'Ah, okay.'

After that, they started thinking football was fun and asking me to play with them. They've gone crazy for the football we play together, individually and with their – and my – respective teams, in video games or on the pitch, and now they're totally fixated.

When they were small they'd been caught in the shadow

of the footballer, but I dragged them out, I took them into the light of the sun, and I made a concerted effort to let only their papa into our home, and never the champion footballer.

In our house in Sweden not a single photograph of me playing football can be seen – not a trophy, nothing. In my children's home only their father lives, not the footballer, because this is our haven, our refuge. They have to grow up independent of my story so that they can write their own stories, so that one day they'll be able to freely choose their own paths, their own challenges.

And their own upside-down revolutionary bicycle kicks, their own turnarounds.

2. Dribbling

(or *About Freedom*)

When I was young I used dribbling as a way to take the mickey out of an opponent. I'd nutmeg the football through his legs, duck around him and then turn and say, 'You see that you won't ever be able to stop me?'

At Ajax I was dribbling all the time. When I was a boy, everything I did was to trick the others.

In particular I studied the Brazilians, both Romário and Ronaldo 'O Fenômeno' ('The Phenomenon') and how they moved the ball forward in a completely different way from everybody else. They pushed it along with tiny taps, never taking their foot off the ball: *thump-thump* . . . outside, inside, lightning-fast . . . *thump-thump*. The same way bandy-players do it – bandy is a kind of ice-hockey that's very popular in Sweden. They move a ball along the ice, tapping it with both sides of the stick, zigzagging forward. And what the Swedes did with a stick, the Brazilians did with their feet. This move – kicking outwards with the outside of the foot, then bringing it back in with the inside of the foot – is known as a flip-flap; it's also known as the 'elástico' and was a move that I loved. It's always been my favourite feint. I used to call it 'the snake', because with a couple of quick taps you slither deviously away, and then you sting like a cobra. *Thump-thump* . . .

The reason I studied the Brazilians was because, sooner or later, they'd always show you something you'd never seen before. And I'd spend hours in the street working on my flip-flap. It's so cool when you get it to work. You might hate an opponent, you might shout insults in their direction from the stand, but when they pull a flip-flap and speed off into the distance, you don't say a thing, you just stand there thinking to yourself: 'Wow, that was spectacular.'

Another trick I liked was the stepover, but I could never manage to be as explosive as Ronaldo. O Fenômeno took off like a cannonball. Who could possibly forget his goal against SS Lazio in the UEFA Cup final in Paris in 1998, which he scored as an Inter player? One feint, then another, then a third. He veers to the right, then he veers to the left, and the goalie Luca Marchegiani heads off in one direction and Ronaldo puts the ball through the goalposts in the opposite direction.

Then I went to play for Juve, and Capello said, 'Dribbling is okay, but what for? To get a shot in, make a move, cross the ball? That's fine. But dribbling just to dribble? That's not right.'

At my age, dribbling has become too costly now. After doing it once I need to recover, because I'm still going to need a store of energy to attack the goal. As Marco van Basten used to like telling me, 'The best thing you can do to help the team is to score goals.'

These days, dribbling is no longer my first choice. I need to husband my strength to get to the goal. I need to keep it simple, and that's the hardest thing to pull off. Pass, shoot: these are the fundamental components of football, which is an elementary sport, however much we might complicate it. What do we say when we see somebody overdoing things with spectacular shots? 'Keep it simple!' In fact the real challenge isn't any special kind of dribbling; it's the simple pass to a teammate, even though your ego is shouting for you to show the world what a phenomenon you really are.

Dribbling is child's play – the same kind of gimmick as popping wheelies on your motorbike to prove what a bad-ass you are. As you grow up, you graduate to a car, with all four wheels planted solidly on the tarmac.

But to me, dribbling was something more: a need for freedom. It was the yearning to run without restraint, to leave everything behind me and tear across the field, all alone, with the wind in my face, an open pitch stretching out before me and my talent on display for the world to see.

When I became Ibra, I'd tell my trainers, 'Okay, you go ahead and work up your schematics and plans, but when it comes to the far end of the pitch, I'll decide what to do.' I've reached a level where I can decide for myself what's best for the team. Roberto Mancini at Inter gave me free rein, but Guardiola at Barcelona didn't.

At Barcelona I was always pre-programmed for every square inch of the pitch, and every fraction of a second of the match. I wasn't myself, because they were telling me where to run and how to run there. I was a prisoner, locked in place.

If you feel you have to tell Ibra what to do, that means you don't really need Ibra. Because you should know, from the outset, that you'll never be able to change him.

It's what I always told Guardiola: 'If you don't like the way I play, then just leave me out of it.' No matter what I said, he kept asking me to defend the post, to go long, to aim for the near post. I can do all that, but that's not the kind of player I am.

At first I did my best to adapt. I made all the effort I could because, after all, it was Guardiola who wanted to bring me on, and it was a wonderful challenge for me. Even before I officially joined the team, I heard everyone saying, 'Ibra isn't the centre forward that Barça needs, he doesn't have the right profile, he won't be able to do it . . .'

So I gave it my all, to prove them wrong and show the people at Barcelona that I was going to be able to become one of them. All the same, every time I had a ball in play, I found that I was second-guessing myself. The first thing I'd think of was my own solution, suggested by my own instinct, but then I'd think of what they wanted me to do. And that went for every word I said and everything I did. I was thinking double and living double. I was no longer myself, for the first time in my life. I held out for six months and then I blew sky-high.

The truth is that Guardiola ought to have found a way to allow me and Messi to play side-by-side, in accordance with our individual strengths. That would have been his job, his profession. But he didn't know how, whereas Luis Enrique figured out the solution, lining up at one fell swoop the trio of Messi, Luis Suárez and Neymar, giving all three of them room to play.

For instance, at Manchester City, Guardiola could have signed Messi, Cristiano Ronaldo and Harry Kane. City would have given him all three. But he didn't want any of them. They were outsized stars, too big for him, with too much personality. 'The Philosopher' prefers players who obey without talking back.

A playbook is good to have, but then you have to take into consideration imagination and sheer quality. If you're convinced that it's your playbook that will win matches for you, then why bother paying for van Basten at all? Just field any old centre forward and he'll do the same job, right? Am I wrong? In fact it's van Basten who gives you trophies to hoist high; he's the champion who wins you matches with his special talents – talents that other players don't possess – but if you want him to display and deploy those talents, then you're going to have to give him the freedom to play.

You'd never tell Neymar to stop dribbling, because that's the essence of his art. It would be like telling a painter not to paint. You'll never tell a fast player to slow down. No, you'll exploit his speed, for the good of the team. The playbook can help to give the team as a collective a certain cohesive form, but the closer an attacker gets to the goal, the more he's going to have to trust his instincts.

A shirt, like a playbook, can turn into a cage that strips you of your freedom.

Staying home and eating the meals that your mother makes for you is nice and comfy, but I've always yearned to walk on fire. I left Sweden to play for Ajax in the Netherlands, and then I went looking for an even bigger challenge. Each time this was the way I saw things: I'm leaving my garden and coming to yours, and I want to see if I'll be able to do the same things as you're doing. If I'm capable, then after a while I'll leave, putting myself to the test again in another garden – each time trying to grow as a person and as a footballer. That's how I became who I am now. I'm not saying that Maldini and Totti, staying at the same club the whole time as they did, were doing what they did out of weakness or fear: not at all, I respect them. And I know that it all depends on our personalities. I find it hard to stay in the same place all my life. I get restless and I feel the need for new challenges.

How can I criticize Hakan Çalhanoğlu's decision to leave Milan and join Inter, considering how many times I've made decisions exactly like that? We should just thank Çalha for the gifts he brought to the team and wish him the best for all his future endeavours.

It sounds bad to say it, and you can't say it was intentional, but Çalha ended up benefiting from a tragic situation. Right in the middle of a match between Denmark and Finland in the 2020 UEFA European Championship, the Danish player Christian Eriksen, who was also at Inter, had a cardiac arrest. And so Inter found itself in need of a player for that position and the door swung open for Hakan. Before that, there had been no offers forthcoming for him, either from Inter or any other club.

46

Hakan is a fantastic kid. He grew and matured immensely, thanks to me. He gained new courage and confidence, and now the only challenge facing him is this: 'Will I be able to achieve the same things without Ibra?' During the UEFA European Championship I regularly texted both him and Ante Rebić: 'It's tough without Ibra, isn't it?' They answered with lots of smiley faces.

Before I arrived, Çalha wasn't performing at anything like the level he achieved afterwards, and Rebić never played. I'd kid Hakan constantly, 'It's all my fault that now you're demanding all sorts of things of Milan, because I made you great.' And I'd tell Ante, 'They renewed your contract, but the credit goes to me, and me alone. Don't forget . . .'

But the deeper truth – playbooks or shirts aside – is that football deprived me of my freedom from the very first day.

First of all, let me make this necessary statement: no one ever put a gun to my head to get me to be a footballer. I made my own decisions, and there's not a thing I wouldn't do all over again in my life. Without football, I'd have been a nobody. I owe everything I have to football. Thanks to the game, I am the man I've become, I live the life that I live, I've seen places and met people. I'll never stop feeling gratitude to my profession.

That said, I've also contributed my fair share to football.

Everyone seems to think that it's fun and easy to be a footballer, but they can't imagine what a burden it is to live a life that's so completely programmed. How do we live? Well, we wake up, we eat breakfast, then we start training, then we eat lunch, then we take a rest and then more training, two matches a week – and so on and so forth, on a continuous loop for fifteen or twenty years. In a Champions League week you might find yourself at a training retreat four days out of every seven. When my sons Maximilian and Vincent were born, that only made matters so much more complicated. I'd stop playing for the national team just so that I could spend more time with them.

When I decided to re-join the national team, for the UEFA European Championship, and the sports journalists at the press conference asked me a question about my sons, I burst into tears. I thought back to the way Vincent wept while I was leaving the house and it hurt me so bad.

There's no doubt about it, footballers make good money, and they take lots of satisfaction from what they do. But most people never think about the fact that while they're living the life of an athlete, which demands great sacrifices, footballers are also missing out on much of what constitutes real life. A footballer's career ends before he turns thirty-five, and then he's no longer the centre of the world's attention; he no longer has to go through his days according to a rigid programme, but finally regains his full personal freedom. All that is certainly true, but he's also no longer twenty years old.

I'm not complaining because I missed going out clubbing or having fun with my friends. No, that's not it at all:

for twenty years I lost the freedom to do what I wanted every day. And, now that I'm forty, I'm a different person entirely. What am I going to do with my life now, after all those sacrifices?

Many footballers fall into a pit of depression when they reach the end of their careers: 'What am I going to do, now that I don't have a daily programme ahead of me?' They're faced with too much freedom – an immense and terrifying sea of time. They can no longer fall back on the compass of a pre-programmed daily life.

I now have an appointment book that tells me: '10 a.m. Milanello, 10.30 a.m. training starts.' Soon that will no longer be the case, I'll no longer have that kind of schedule. So what will I do? I'll take the boys to school. And then what? Will I just sit there, waiting for them to come back out? No, I'll go to the gym to work out for a while: half an hour or an hour of high-intensity training. *Boom, boom, boom* . . . And then what? For twenty years we've felt alive, thanks to the adrenaline that filled us, out on the pitch, playing in front of thousands of fans. Now we're going to have to find some other kind of adrenaline, a different form. It isn't easy.

Lots of former players go on TV as commentators. I can tell you why they do it: they need the attention. They don't need the money, they need the attention. For years now you've had 80,000 people at a time following everything you did at the stadium, as well as all the sports journalists writing about you. Then you stop playing and, all at once, you have nothing. So that's when you decide you can become a commentator. I'm not interested in that. I have no need for attention. At the level I've reached, I'll get plenty of attention, no matter what I do.

At some point in the future I could become a coach. After all, I'm already helping young players and the team as a whole to grow, but to judge from the coaches I've had, it's a profession that involves plenty of stress. So I don't know; we'll see. In any case, it's something that demands a period of study and preparation. Having been a great player doesn't necessarily mean that you'll be able to become a great coach. To distinguish yourself in that field it's not enough to know how to play. Now you have to know how to transfer your own ideas into the heads of the other guys who are playing for you – and that's the hard part. That's where you'll notice the difference between a really good coach and a mediocre one.

You need to start by coaching young people, or maybe in a lower league. You have to learn by making mistakes, building up experience and then slowly climbing to the top of the heap and, once there, you'll no longer be able to afford any more mistakes. I would never start by coaching at a major club, the way Pirlo did with Juve, because I'd have so much to lose. Even if I started winning right away, I'd learn nothing, because the only way you learn is by falling on your face – by losing. If you hope to grow, then you need to have room to make mistakes at the start.

I don't know what I'll do tomorrow with my freedom, but I do know that, for now, I don't feel like a fully free man.

Let's say I decide to leave home and go out for a walk. I won't be able to go a hundred yards without having people bothering me. And if there are people bothering you, then you have no freedom. I don't know if I'll ever be able to have that kind of freedom in my life. Actually I don't expect I will. Because I've pushed the work I do to such a high level, I'll be paying the price for many years to come. Where do I feel free? In nature, when I go into the forest or the woods, where the animals have no idea who I am. But even there the animals are likely to recognize me . . . because I'm an animal, just like they are.

I feel free on a little island in the middle of Lake Malar in eastern Sweden, and even more so in my woods, along the border with Norway. It's a remote forest in the mountains, in the far north, where I have a small cottage without electricity or running water, a place you can only reach by snowmobile in the winter. More than 2,500 acres of land. To give you some idea, the Trafford Park Estate – which houses Old Trafford – is only twenty acres. For miles and miles there's no risk whatsoever of encountering another human being.

Now that's where I feel truly free. I also feel free when I'm out on my boat, but I never entirely trust the sea. I don't know what's lurking beneath the surface. In the forest, on the other hand, I have total control of the situation. But I can't live there all the time, among the trees, far away from everybody else: I'd lose my mind.

Lots of people say that footballers have such a great life. Sure, there's plenty of adrenaline, you sign contracts, people tell you that you're the greatest. But when you quit, there's nothing left. There's no more adrenaline, there's no one left to stroke your ego. At most, they might tell you that you used to be the best there was. Not the best there *is*, only the best there *was*. When you're playing and you need something, you ask for it and they'll bring it to you. After you've stopped playing, you ask for something and they'll tell you, 'Okay, come and get it.' They turn off the pinball machine. The little silver ball falls right into the hole. The tilt sign goes off, the buzzer sounds.

I'm afraid of quitting because I don't know what awaits me afterwards. Every day that goes by, I get a little closer to that moment and I start to realize that I'm afraid – more and more afraid. It's not a matter of money. I'll have plenty of that. It's a very different problem: what am I going to do with myself? It won't be long until both my boys turn eighteen and strike out on their own. What will I do then? That's what makes me uncomfortable. I thought I'd be ready to quit and devote myself to other things, but instead the more time passes, the more I worry.

When I come to the end of my career I'll have to find the adrenaline that surges through me now when I battle against Chiellini. But where will I find it? I can't exactly go out into the street and pick fights with perfect strangers. I'm not a nut. Should I go into business? That could be a healthy challenge: if it works, it would be a real jackpot, but that's still not the kind of adrenaline that makes me feel alive.

I feel free when I'm able to dress comfortably.

I loathe having to put on a suit and tie. It forces you to become arrogant and obnoxious. You go into a restaurant dressed like that and it's as if you are telling everyone, 'Just look at how important I am.' I don't care what other people think of me. Of course, no two ways about it: if I have to do it, I'll do it. On official occasions I don't feel comfortable dressed in all that fancy attire, with a bow tie choking me and all the rest, but if I've had to do it, I've done it. I only feel free when I'm dressed casually, when I feel comfortable. When I'm wearing a tracksuit.

My cars give me freedom, too.

I like them, but I didn't buy them to show off the fact that I can afford them. I haven't washed them in years. I don't buy them to show them off; I buy them for the adrenaline that pumps into my blood when I drive them on the motorway. My cars give me the confidence that I can escape whenever I choose to, because they are fast and no one else can catch them. In that sense, they are my freedom. I know that I can roar away at any given moment.

When I went back to Milan I had no car of my own. I had a couple of cars sent down, precisely because I was missing the adrenaline of freedom. People say to me, 'Zlatan, it's more fun to take your car to a racetrack and hit top speed, like a Formula One racer.' No, that bores me. I'd feel like a hamster running on a treadmill. I much prefer the motorway, because I need to get away from other people.

When people recognize me, they even follow me in cars, not just on foot in search of selfies. That's when I put the pedal to the metal in my Ferrari, which can accelerate from zero to 300 kph (185 mph) in fifteen seconds. Don't get me wrong; I'm not saying that I ever go at 300 kph . . . Anyway, I hit the accelerator and roar off down the road.

Covid took away the freedom that I did have and changed me as a person. I was far from my family when I got sick in 2020. I found myself shut up in my apartment as if I were in prison. I felt alone against the world. Physically I wasn't feeling so bad, but I simply wasn't used to this kind of situation. I had always had my family close to me, especially if I wasn't in good health. Among other things, that was a particularly delicate period of my life because I had some very important decisions to make: should I quit or go on playing? I couldn't say whether I'd be capable of staying in Milan all alone for the next six months. I even talked it over with team management at Milan, but I didn't want to turn it into a problem for Maldini or Pioli. It was a matter that concerned me, and me alone.

Covid changed so many people. Personally, I'm perfectly comfortable staying home, but I still like to get out every now and then. For a whole year we couldn't do that. When they relaxed the restrictions and I went out to dinner at a restaurant again, a wave of panic washed over me. I told my friends, 'Let's eat up quickly, because I want to go home.'

I was no longer used to being out and about. I saw too many people gathered around me and I felt uncomfortable, but this time it wasn't because I'm a famous celebrity and people were pestering me. It was because I had changed: something that was perfectly normal – a crowded restaurant – now struck me as abnormal, whereas the abnormal had become normal. I was struggling to breathe and I felt deeply uncomfortable. 'Come on, hurry up, I want to get out of here.'

None of my friends understood. 'What are you talking about, Zlatan? The pandemic is over. Let's enjoy ourselves!'

I don't know if that's really freedom.

Another spectacular form of dribbling was the motorcycle ride I took to get to the studio in time to take part in the first evening of the Sanremo Music Festival of 2021. For those who don't know, this is a hugely popular televised song contest in Italy, which started in 1951 and inspired the Eurovision Song Contest. It's massive.

So once that day's training is done, we leave Milanello aboard a minibus. It's early afternoon; we have plenty of time to get there. My first scheduled appearance at Sanremo is at eight that evening, a promo on RAI – Italian state television – to launch the festival's opening. But then, at a certain point, we wind up stuck in traffic, at a dead halt. The traffic jam gets worse and worse, and my driver turns on the radio in search of information. A truck was involved in an accident and swerved round, blocking the road; there's even been a death. Two hours later we're still sitting there. Time passes, and the stress intensifies. They call us from the festival, worried and concerned, and I ask them if they can send a police squad car to escort us to Sanremo. They tell me that the festival is too much in the public eye, and that sort of special treatment would become a major news story and a scandal.

I'm more and more on edge, so I get out of the mini-bus and start walking through the lines of stalled cars. After sitting in one place for six hours, I can't take it any more. I look at my watch. I'm going to miss the first night of the festival entirely.

So I go back to the minibus and tell my assistant, 'Give me your jacket and track me with the GPS. Keep tabs on where I'm going on your mobile. Okay?'

I stop a scooter that's threading its way through the cars. This is the kind of situation that demands a stroke of luck. And luck is exactly what I have.

The driver recognizes me immediately. 'Ibrahimović . . . I'm a Milan fan.'

'Excellent. Get me to Sanremo fast.'

'But that's nowhere near here.'

'I absolutely have to get there.'

He lends me the spare helmet that he's carrying in his luggage box and we take off. For the first twenty minutes I trace the route on my mobile, because I have no idea who this guy is. For all I know, he might kidnap me and take me who-knows-where. No, it looks like he's taking exactly the right route. Excellent – we're heading straight for San-remo. So I film myself on the back of the scooter, to have some evidence, because I know that when I tell the story no one's going to believe it. The poor guy is going slowly because he's clearly terrified. I understand that: he's trans-porting Ibra's legs, and one of those legs is already in bad shape to start with. He's driving slowly and fishtailing, because I'm a lot of extra weight to carry.

'Let me drive,' I suggest.

He's not willing to do that.

My assistant back on the minibus is terrified, too, because he's lost track of my signal on the GPS and is afraid that I've had a crash. All that's happened, though, is that we've gone through a long tunnel. The signal comes back.

When we get to Sanremo, I'm frozen solid. I've just spent an hour on the back of a motorcycle, without gloves, wearing nothing but a light jacket for warmth, a helmet without a visor, and nothing covering my face but a surgical mask to ward off Covid.

I thank the guy and he tells me, 'Now I can admit it: that's the first time I've ever taken my scooter out on the motorway.'

Then why on earth didn't he let me drive? I was ready to eat him alive. Instead I thanked him again. 'You were great. Wait for my assistants – they'll be here hopefully before too long. You can ask them for anything you want.'

He answers, 'All I want is a selfie.'

When I get to the Ariston Theatre in Sanremo, I'm a terrifying sight. One eye is bloodshot, and my lips are so cold they're blue. I stand close to a floodlight to warm up and then they decide, 'You can't go onstage looking like that, Zlatan. We're changing the line-up. You can go on later. Just relax and try to get warm.'

For another hour I stay in the bathroom, blasting hot air at myself with the blow-drier and eating a couple of slices of bresaola. At last I go out onstage.

One of Italy's most famous TV presenters is known as 'Amadeus'. He's one of the hosts this year. He shows the video I recorded (you can watch it online) and I tell the story of my trip through the traffic – and that's the beginning of the festival.

I ran a considerable risk, because I could easily have been injured, and I already had an injury. My motorcyclist, new to motorway driving, might have taken a wrong turn or driven me somewhere else. I acted in defiance of all caution and logic. But when I set my mind to something, I take it all the way – it's stronger than me.

Now, let's take a step back.

In the summer, I had a phone call from someone asking, 'Zlatan, would you like to appear as a guest at the Sanremo Music Festival?'

Like you, I don't even know what the Sanremo Music Festival is at this point. I ask, 'Has anyone else ever done this before?' I'm given a long list of prestigious guests. But if it's nothing more than a brief appearance, why should I bother? I give it a shot: 'If you want me, I'm going to have to appear every night of the festival.'

They counter, 'Okay, you can be the third MC, along with Amadeus and Fiorello, for all five evenings of the festival.' (Fiorello is another well-known Italian TV presenter who goes by one name only – think of the pair of them like an Italian Ant and Dec . . .)

Then I ask, 'Has anyone else ever done this?'
Never.

'Excellent. If I'm the first guy to do it, then I'm in. But hold on, because I'm negotiating my new contract with Milan.'

Negotiations for the renewal of my contract drag out

ad infinitum and look like they'll never end. Finally I make up my mind: if I sit here waiting for Milan, I could miss out on lots of opportunities.

I pick up the phone and call the Sanremo people. 'I've decided. I'm coming to the festival.' I figure that if I wind up signing a contract with Milan, then I'll just add a clause stating that they have to give me a week off, without specifying when or why. That's partly because I have a requirement from Sanremo to say nothing about my involvement with the show. That absolutely has to remain a secret. I can tell no one.

Okay, so I'm going to the festival, but what am I actually going to be doing?

I'd never seen the festival before. I would ask everyone I knew and I always got the same answer: 'Sanremo is the most prestigious and important music show that exists in Italy.' There's not really an equivalent in the UK. This is on a whole other scale from TV shows like *X Factor* or *The Voice* – it's more like headlining Glastonbury.

Now this is the right occasion to say thank you to the people of Italy, to express my gratitude for everything they've given me, because I owe it all to Italy that I am who – and what – I am today. It's thanks to Italy that the whole world knows me. I had already played for Ajax, but my real career started in Turin in 2004, when Mino Raiola brought me to Juve.

The day of the Sanremo Festival draws closer. I keep the secret, but the people at RAI are a little less cautious. They leak my name to stir up curiosity, expectations and marketing interest. At that point I'm forced to talk about it with Pioli: 'Coach, you know that week off I insisted on putting into the contract? Well, I'll be going to Sanremo.'

'Fine,' is all he says.

Stefano immediately checks the championship fixture list. The second evening of the festival coincides with the midweek Milan–Udinese match. He's no longer saying, 'Fine.'

I talk it over with Paolo Maldini. Everyone has the utmost respect for my decision – they know that there are signed contracts. No one thinks of criticizing me, but inside I feel a burning flame. I have too many responsibilities towards my teammates, I'm their leader: I can't abandon them, I can't skip a championship match for a music festival.

I pick up the phone and call my contact at Sanremo. 'Listen, I'm not coming for the second evening. I'm happy to pay the penalty and anything else you want, but I can't abandon my teammates, because they're why I came to Milan in the first place. They're my first concern.'

They understand and are very cooperative.

'It's not a problem, Zlatan, we'll come up with some solution.' The plan is for me to go to Sanremo with a trainer and a physio, to work out and sleep aboard my boat, so that I can stay as calm and relaxed as possible, and then show up for the match. Instead, what happens is that I get injured at the Stadio Olimpico playing against Roma: a sprain.

At that point the people at Sanremo assume that the problem has been taken care of: I won't be able to play against Udinese, so I'll be able to go to Sanremo, since

I won't have to be at the San Siro. But it's not that simple. Even if I won't be out on the pitch, I'm still my team-mates' leader. I can't have my guys thinking I'm somewhere else. In fact I go to the stadium, and that evening I do a live feed from my house to Sanremo.

The people at the festival were great. They never put any pressure on me, they didn't give me scripts or scenarios to study, they demanded nothing of me. They never caused any stress. All they ever told me was: 'Just be yourself.'

That struck me as so very strange . . . If what everyone was telling me was true and this was Italy's most important music show, then I expected to be asked to do something special, even if it was only being a clown. Instead: 'We just need you to be Zlatan Ibrahimović.'

'And that's all?' I asked. 'That and nothing more?'

'Yes, that's all.'

With Amadeus I immediately achieved an incredible chemistry. He told me, 'You just go out onstage and I'll follow you.' What the . . . ? This is your show – I'm the one who ought to be following you. 'No,' Amadeus insists. 'You're the pilot and I'm the co-pilot.'

We rehearse our entrance onto the stage at the Ariston Theatre and the band strikes up the Champions League theme music.

'What is that supposed to be?' I ask right away.

'You're a champion and this is the theme music of champions,' they explain.

'No, that's an insult, because I've never won the Champions League. Do you really want me to be myself? Then I'll give you a song to play.'

So I gave them *'Jutro je'* by the Serbo-Bosnian singer Nada Topčagić, a cheerful song that I remember from my childhood, a piece I'd danced to at my home with my staff, during the party celebrating my 500th career goal. And every time I came out onstage they put on that Slavic music – the same music that was later played at the San Siro Stadium, too, while Milan was warming up. That song became a real Sanremo classic. So I was being myself to an even greater degree. I felt absolutely at ease.

All credit is due to Amadeus, who never tired of telling me, 'Just go out onstage and do what you want. If you make a mistake, keep going. Don't let it stop you. Go on ahead. I'll follow behind you. Improvise, and don't be afraid.'

That's exactly what I did, and I was having the time of my life. Like on the pitch, really: there was a general sense of playfulness that everyone was sticking to. I would jump in, making things up and improvising freely.

I have to say the chemistry wasn't as strong with Fiorello, because it was always unpredictable – I never knew what was going to happen. He was the first pilot, but also pilot numbers two and three, then I was pilot number four, and last of all came Amadeus, pilot number five. When Fiorello came onstage I was in a defensive stance, I let him run the show, in part because the way he speaks Italian is just too fast. One time at lunch I even told him so: 'Fiorello, slow down, don't talk so fast! I can't understand a thing you're saying . . .' So the next evening, to make fun of me, he started speaking slowly and enunciating every syllable.

There may be some people who think I seemed arrogant, because backstage, during the live show, the singers would come and ask me to take selfies, and I'd reject their requests, saying, 'Not right now!' I wasn't doing that because I was putting on airs. It was because I was focused on the show, the timing of the various entrances onstage. When I'm working, I work. Selfies come later.

Later on, though, things went south. A storm of controversy burst out in the newspapers – I was fined by UEFA for having a financial stake in Bethard, a Malta-based betting company. Then I was wrongly sent off in the game at Parma. After that I got injured – a sprain – I went back to playing, and I was injured again. I got a new physio and, before I knew it, he came down with Covid.

When I arrived in Sanremo I was in top form. But then the situation started to deteriorate. I'm not superstitious, but there are times when you have to stop and think. And I thought about it all right, long and hard: either Sanremo or Lukaku must have cast some kind of spell on me. But we will talk about Lukaku later.

Still, taking part in the festival was fantastic, all things considered. Everyone seemed to have gone into a wild frenzy. The RAI executives, backstage, were following the viewing audience numbers in real time. They noticed that every time I went onstage there was a spike in viewers, so they started shouting, 'Send out Ibra! Send out Ibra!' They completely rearranged the schedule. I was only supposed to come out a couple of times each night, but instead they kept sending me out onstage and telling me to improvise.

The more time I spent onstage, the more confident I became and the more fun I was having. In fact I felt like saying, 'Listen, Amadeus, why don't you just stay in your dressing room and let me MC the whole show . . .'

It was becoming my show, instead of his.

But the most gratifying sensation of all was the knowledge that I'd finally changed my image entirely in the eyes of the larger audience – that I'd risen to a different level of popularity and approval. Thanks to my appearances, for the first time I felt I was now appreciated and accepted by everyone: Inter fans and Juventus fans, Milan fans and Napoli fans; I was no longer someone standing under the banner of one club, but instead was someone who was broadly loved, with a shared popularity among all Italians. People often judge you before they know you. Now I feel as if every Italian knows me, at least a little.

All the people I met after the show saw me as Ibra of Sanremo, not Ibra of AC Milan.

I go to Pinzolo, in the Trentino region, to do some mountain-biking in the woods, and I meet an elderly couple out hiking. The woman tells me, 'Ibra, you were fantastic at Sanremo.' On the beach, in Sardinia, something very similar happens. Another grandmother: 'Ibra, you were fantastic and very likeable on TV. You even know how to smile.'

These were compliments that sent me to the moon, because I hadn't earned them on the pitch with my athletic talent; I won them just by being myself, showing the world my true self. According to my philosophy, this is perfection: being yourself.

I sang a song onstage with Bologna boss Siniša Mihajlović. You can watch it online, if you really want to. When I did that, I didn't worry about coming off looking good. I didn't rehearse to make the best possible appearance: I improvised, I sang flat and off-key, but I let them see the real me. So I was perfect.

Once the lockdown was lifted after the pandemic, I walked into a restaurant and everyone broke into applause. Okay, maybe they'd have done the same thing a year earlier, but that evening I got the distinct sensation they weren't applauding the god of the San Siro, but rather the man of Sanremo.

3. The Opponent
(*or About War*)

At the start of my career my head was like a live bomb. All it took was a shock to make it explode. My opponents picked up on this right away and did their best to take advantage of the fact, provoking me to the best of their abilities.

While I was playing for Juventus, too, with a substantial chunk of my career already under my belt, I could still lose control, if things lined up the right way. A match against Bayern Munich, for instance.

Michael Ballack targeted me from the get-go: harsh words, insults, fouls when the ball was miles away.

I fell for it. Two yellow cards and I was off. I grew up after that.

Someone offered me a little advice: 'Zlatan, change the direction of your anger. Don't aim it against your opponent or the referee. Pour it into your game instead. Put more of your anger into your football and you'll see: you'll wind up enjoying your revenge against the players who work to get under your skin, instead of getting yourself sent off.'

Back in the Malmö ghetto where I grew up, if someone said something to me, I was practically obliged to answer back. If I ran into some guy who asked me, 'The fuck you looking at?' I would always respond, 'The fuck *you* looking at?'

Out on the street, where I come from, that's the way things work. There were very specific codes you had to follow. And I took those codes of behaviour out onto the pitch with me. First we'd lash out at each other with words, then we'd get into closer proximity to see which of us was the strongest, both mentally and physically.

I was young, and I reacted instinctively because I still lacked self-control, whereas the experienced players were doing it intentionally, to get under my skin. Like Siniša Mihajlović in that Inter–Juventus match in 2012. He started insulting me the minute the referee's whistle blew. At a certain point I gave him a head-butt that got me sent off. I'd fallen for it again.

Mihajlović didn't hate me, he had nothing against me personally. He was only looking to gain some advantage for his team and to win the match.

Marco Materazzi was a very different matter. He came in looking to hurt you. Leaving aside the interests at play in the match, he had his own personal strategy to get on his opponent's nerves.

When someone's not really all that good at the game, they'll use anything they can come up with, to get an edge. That was his style. But if you do certain things to me, I'm not going to forget, because it sticks right here, in the chest, and I don't let it go. I waited five years until I was able to get back at him.

Juventus–Inter, 2 October 2005: Materazzi wore those special Nike contact lenses that were popular at the time and changed your eye colour. I remember a pair of raging red irises, like the eyes of a savage beast, stalking me everywhere I turned. He tackles me successfully, both feet extended in a scissor. I'm forced to leave the pitch so that the doctors can tend to me. I limp off. Capello wants to field a substitute, but I tell him, 'No, Coach. I can do this.'

I get back onto the pitch with one aim only: to track Materazzi down. At this point it isn't about football any more. As far as I'm concerned, the match is already over. But I can't even walk for the pain. Capello can tell, and he calls me off the field.

I wait for my chance.

This is how things work in my world: you never forget, and you wait patiently for the right time to take revenge. I told myself over and over: 'When I get my hands on him, I'll hurt him badly – so badly that he'll remember what he did to me. And I'll take my revenge in the light of day, making my motives and intentions perfectly clear to everyone.'

We faced off in other matches, but the right moment never arrived. I wasn't interested in letting fly with a good hard kick, just for the brute thrill of the thing, and then leaving. No, I had to see the perfect opportunity for what I had in mind.

Then I transfer to Inter.

Now Materazzi and I are teammates, so I have to put my plan on hold. I can't lash out at him during training. That's not something I'd do. Right now we have to play together and win together.

I've always shown complete respect for my teammates. I even have conversations with Materazzi from time to time, and I know him as a person, but in my mind, the memory remains as clear as ever. I haven't forgotten, I haven't set it aside. In fact I have an incredibly good memory. For example, one day a little boy gave me a T-shirt to autograph and I told him, 'I autographed it once before, last year, in Rome.' His jaw dropped.

I play for Inter for three years, and then I leave for Barcelona under Guardiola. Time passes. I go back to Milan, this time to play in the red-and-black shirt of AC Milan. Then it's the week of the derby – the first derby of the season. The newspapers and everyone in the business start pumping up the challenge. Everyone is writing about Materazzi vs Ibra, but I'm perfectly relaxed. I'm concentrating on the match. My Milan team absolutely has to win this game in order to hold on to its place at the top, which it's just achieved by overtaking Lazio.

We're playing at their stadium, so Inter fans are in a majority and they're whistling and taunting, but that's merely an advantage as far as I'm concerned, because it jacks up the amount of adrenaline circulating in my bloodstream, making me feel stronger.

Sunday 12 November 2010: game on. I find myself facing off against Lúcio, Materazzi and Iván Córdoba, three tough defenders I know well. At our first clash they mass against me in a small herd and immediately make it clear exactly what kind of match I should expect from them. Okay, cards-on-the-table time. I'll have to keep my eyes wide open and not get distracted for so much as a second. A high-lofted ball comes dropping straight down, I tense for the leap, but realize that Materazzi and Lúcio are converging on the spot – one from the left, the other from the right – and aim to catch me between them. I act like I'm springing into the air, but instead remain with both feet on the ground and watch as they smash into each other. Fun!

Every single move goes like that: a battle. In part that's because, as an Inter player, I'd clashed with the kop. After a goal I'd taunted them, grabbing my genitals, and now the Inter fans, seeing me in the red-and-black shirt, view me as a traitor and are dying to witness my execution.

There have been only a few minutes of play. I see a long, arcing ball coming my way, I run and I enter the penalty area. Materazzi cuts me down from behind: penalty. I score the penalty, then I throw both arms wide and stand there, staring at the Inter ultras as they vomit waves of insults in my direction. Adrenaline surging – the way I like it. It's great.

At the start of the second half I see the moment arrive, a moment I've been awaiting for the past five years. There's a ball midway between me and Materazzi. I know that he'll come in, looking to hurt me. But he doesn't realize that I have something far worse planned for him, because my anger has been building up for a long, long time.

He's in the ideal situation to make it look like a simple clash of competition, fighting to win control of the ball, which lies exactly halfway between us. He comes sliding in, both feet forward, and I jump to avoid an impact. If I'd come sliding in feet-first as well, we'd each have had a 50 per cent shot: either he'd have hit me or I'd have hit him. Instead I become airborne. I tuck up my knees and, as he slides beneath me, I hit him hard in the head with my elbow. I hear the flat crack of impact and his groan of pain: 'Aaargh . . .'

I could roll on the ground and pretend I'd been badly hurt in the clash myself. Instead I stand up as if nothing has happened and walk away. Materazzi remains on the ground and they take him off to the hospital for a precautionary check-up. I know I hit him hard, right in the temple.

Dejan Stanković, who is a friend, comes to see me and asks, 'Why did you do it, Zlatan?'

I answer him, 'Because I've waited five years for the chance. Forget about it, Dejan. Now beat it.'

Among the most euphoric players in the dressing room is Pippo Inzaghi: 'The finest derby in my life: 1–0 for us, a tackle by Ibra, and Materazzi in hospital!'

With one blow, I'd also taken revenge for all the nasty tackles suffered by Pippo and Andriy Shevchenko in the preceding derbies.

The next day I had to catch a plane back to Milan Linate Airport. I'm told, 'Materazzi's on that flight.'

I answer, 'Fine. Let's see what he does.'

I get up from my seat. Maybe he'll front up to me. I hope so. Let me see what kind of a man you are, Matrix. Instead he walks past me without a word.

Now I know how easy it is to hide behind an Instagram account, make your points in interviews, post a picture of the European Cup and write, 'Ibra, do you have this?' It just makes me laugh. I don't need to indulge in gimmicks like that. I did what I had to do when the time was right, man-to-man. I don't have any outstanding grudges left with Materazzi.

One day I asked Capello, 'Coach, here at Juve there are lots of champions. How do you earn the respect of all these men?'

He answered me, 'I don't ask for it, I take it.'

I never asked Materazzi for respect, I took it for myself. In my own way.

By the way, speaking of derby challenges, Romelu Lukaku made me laugh when he proclaimed himself 'the true king of Milan'. He never caught me with a nasty tackle, but I'm going to make him eat the words he said to me on the field.

In a year at Manchester United he never once opened his mouth, he was as good as a little lamb; but when he got to Italy, the journalists convinced him that he had become a top player and he decided that he was the king.

Lukaku isn't a bad person, but he made a serious mistake: he turned against me.

In my second year at Man U I was badly injured. I wasn't playing and I was only receiving 20 per cent of my salary. Every opportunity looked like a good chance to earn some cash, so I launched a challenge. We were at lunch before a match: 'Listen, Romelu, every time you fail to control the ball with one touch, you give me fifty pounds. All right?'

'But what if I get it right?' he asked me.

'I promise that I'm going to make you stronger. Come on, Rom, let me become a millionaire.'

He laughed. He really thought he was a first-class player, but every time he failed to control a ball, then he'd have to chase after it.

But don't be misled. My challenge, which I felt certain I was going to win, was also a way of helping Lukaku to see what he needed to work on in order to improve. I was helping him. And in fact he matured and grew. Today he's a much stronger player than he was at Man U. But while he never challenged me when he was playing in England, the minute he set foot in Italy, he came for me, proclaiming that he was now 'the true king of Milan'.

Evidently he hadn't fully learned the law of the jungle: if you want to be the new lion king, you have to make sure you've killed the old one.

Then comes the championship derby: February 2021. Milan wins it with two goals from me, and I announce on social media, 'Milan has never had a king, just a god.'

One month later we meet up on opposing sides in the Coppa Italia.

Lukaku is arguing with Alessio Romagnoli, the captain. Okay, that can happen. We all argue from time to time. It's a derby, so the tension is high out on the pitch. But then he starts arguing with Alexis Saelemaekers, too.

My team is too young – it's not like my old Milan team. If you tried to go up against Gattuso, he'd kill you. So I tell myself: 'It's time for you to weigh in here, Zlatan. The guys aren't afraid, but if they're not careful, it will be their downfall.'

I take Lukaku aside and I tell him in English, 'Keep your mouth shut and stay in your place.'

He comes back with, 'What'll you do if I don't?'

I look at him in surprise: is this guy talking to me?

He says it again. 'What'll you do if I don't?'

I explain to him in English: '*I'm gonna break every bone in your body if you open your mouth.*'

He steps forward.

According to street rules, you can come close only up to a certain point, after which I'm bound to defend myself. I push my head against his and shove him backwards. Lukaku starts insulting my wife, and then I go for his Achilles heel: his mother's voodoo.

When he went from Everton to Manchester United, it was claimed that a voodoo ritual performed by his mother had convinced him it was time to change clubs. Lukaku had denied it, but in my world, a guy is supposed to have the balls to simply announce that he wants to go and play for Man U, without inventing a bunch of tall tales.

I say to him, 'Go tell your mother to do a voodoo spell for you.'

Here he basically loses it. 'What did you just say about my mother? What did you say?'

Nothing. I haven't insulted him. The first half comes to an end.

According to Covid regulations, we aren't allowed to leave the pitch together; each team has to take its own tunnel back to the dressing room. But I exit the field along with the Inter players. The TV broadcasts footage of Lukaku and me side-by-side, with me smiling.

I'm telling him, 'Come on down here with me, and let me have my fun.' And I think to myself: 'In the tunnel no one will be able to see us.'

I head down, I wait for him, but I see him still up there, lingering, his progress blocked by Nicolò Barella. By little Barella? A giant like you? That must mean that you're really not all that eager to catch up with me.

Lukaku threatens me from a distance. 'I'm going to put three bullets in your head!'

What am I supposed to do now?

I reply to him, 'Once you're done watching that movie in your head, come and see me.'

The Inter players send me away, saying to me, 'We know what you have in mind, Zlatan. You're trying to rile him.'

A friend of mine who plays for Inter confided to me, 'Lukaku has a hard time with you. When you gave your teammates a gift, he did the same with his guys just a few days later. Anything you do, he copies.'

I go to our dressing room. I remember that Paolo Maldini was also standing by the door. I'm the first to leave, and I wait for Lukaku to go by. When he does, I clap very slowly as if to say, 'Well, here I am, waiting for you. What are we going to do about it?'

He responds with applause of his own and heads straight out onto the pitch. Unfortunately, in the second half I get a second yellow card and I'm sent off. But I keep my temper. I had the situation totally under control. I was no longer the rash kid who exploded at the slightest provocation.

After that derby, things started going badly for me: sending-off, defeat, the widely reported controversies about the betting company, injuries, my physio's Covid . . .

At first I thought the Sanremo Music Festival had brought me bad luck. But could it have been that Lukaku had performed some voodoo ritual to hurt me?

In my mind, I decided that I had to settle things with Lukaku out on the pitch, the same way I had done with Materazzi. Unfortunately he left Serie A and we didn't come up against Chelsea in the Champions League. But there will be other opportunities . . .

There are many different types of opponent. The tough but fair opponent. The opponent who's out to hurt you. The opponent who acts like a bully on the field, because he knows that if a brawl breaks out there's never really going to be a proper scrap, because the referee and your teammates will weigh in. The opponent who isn't afraid to settle scores in the dressing room.

But the scariest ones are the well-behaved, relaxed players who turn into raging banshees when they finally lose control. They're the most dangerous because you don't know what to expect from them – you never know what they're capable of.

One example: Francesco Toldo.

Francesco is the nicest person in the world, kind and always cheerful. In my imagination, he wouldn't be capable of hurting a fly.

Then comes that brawl in Valencia in 2007, during a Champions League match.

Toldo tries to separate Nicolás Burdisso from the Spaniards but, as he's holding him back, along comes that consummate gentleman David Navarro and hauls him off and punches him in the nose, smashing it so that it's off to one side. I get goosebumps just thinking back on it.

Francesco, who feels at fault, heads down to the dressing room and walks towards the Spaniards' dressing room. There are fifteen people in ahead of him. I think to myself: 'The first Spaniard he meets is going to send him back to us, wrapped up with a bow.' Instead, Toldo ploughs right through them. There's not one of them capable of stopping him, not even the security guards.

Toldo bursts into the Valencia dressing room, searching for that coward, who locks himself into the bathroom, quaking in terror. You need to be very cautious when dealing with someone like Francesco.

Another unlikely individual of that sort was Patrick Vieira, at a Bayern Munich–Juve match.

Mark van Bommel plays dirty, hits hard, talks freely and tries to get under your skin. He decides to target Patrick, who doesn't say a word about it on the pitch, but then at the end of the match – so discreetly that nobody notices – he leaves our dressing room and walks into Bayern's, all alone, to teach Van Bommel there are things you just don't do.

You never wanted to provoke someone like Patrick. Better to leave him be.

Nesta, Fabio Cannavaro, Lilian Thuram, Thiago Silva – I've never been afraid of the defenders who hit me hard; only of the ones who kept me from laying eyes on the ball.

When I was passed the ball, it was up to me to decide which direction to go, yet when I got there, they were already waiting for me, with the ball between their feet. The fact that I was more powerful than them, with greater technical ability, did nothing for me in terms of outrunning their sheer speed of thought.

Silva might have been the most capable of them all, but that's not to minimize Nesta's qualities: brilliance, stamina and personality.

During training at Milanello, Nesta challenged me and motivated me. If I scored a goal against him in one of our training games, he'd minimize it: 'You were just lucky' or, 'I must have made a mistake.' He didn't want to make me feel too good about myself, and he refused to acknowledge my achievements. That would wind me up so that I'd give it my all, and we would both train well.

But if I have to choose the two central pillars of my ideal team, I'd have to say Thuram and Cannavaro, because they were an unbeatable duo: both of them as tough as nails, joined at the hip, thinking with one brain, completing each other, assisting each other, together comprising a single, solid block of marble.

A manager can't hit you with a sliding tackle, but he does have ways of stopping you.

Crossing paths with Mourinho, for instance, is always a spectacular experience. When I faced off with him, I was playing for PSG, and he was with Chelsea. He talked at me throughout the whole match. Mou can put you in more awkward situations than any of his players.

It annoys me not to know what he told Guardiola that time he came up behind him and spoke into his ear, during the semi-final match in the 2010 Champions League between Barcelona and Inter.

I was at the side of the pitch, ready to go on. Guardiola, next to me, was giving me the final tactical instructions. José left the Inter dugout, came up behind us and whispered something to Pep, to get on his nerves. I still wonder what he told him. I was too focused on the match and I didn't overhear it.

Mou is terrifying. It's nice to see him in Italy again, now that he's head coach at Roma.

Gattuso would also get me worked up as a coach.

When I faced off against him in Naples with my Milan team, we had good fun. Each of us stung the other, to our mutual amusement. I would say to him, 'Come on, Rino, sit down, try to behave there on the bench.'

And he'd shoot back, 'Shut up, you dirty Slav.'

And I'd shoot back, 'Why don't *you* shut up, before I deck you.'

Playing against Rino is always a spectacular experience, as it was when we were teammates at Milan; he'd play pranks on me, and I'd stuff him upside down into rubbish bins, but everybody knows those stories by now.

Massimiliano Allegri has changed a great deal since I knew him, ten years ago. He's gained in confidence and range, and he always speaks with great self-assurance.

I remember the match AC Milan played in London against Arsenal in 2012.

In the first leg we won 4–0; for the second-leg Max brought two goalies to warm the bench, because the CEO of Milan, Adriano Galliani, had just watched a match where the first and second goalies were injured and the team didn't have a third on hand. Basically it was a way of warding off bad luck.

We lose, 3–0, an embarrassing result that puts us on the brink of elimination, but in the dressing room Allegri seems pleased and contented.

In front of everyone, I shout at him, 'Oh, so you're happy, are you? How the hell can you be satisfied with a 3–0 defeat?'

He answers me, 'Why don't you worry about your own responsibilities, because you were a fucking disgrace on the pitch.'

And I retort, 'You're the fucking disgrace – bringing two goalies along with you just to warm the bench!'

Saying things right to each other's face is always the best approach. Relations between us have remained friendly, straightforward and based on a great and abiding respect. Now it impresses me to see Max so self-confident and even arrogant, in the best sense of the word. At press conferences he always talks with his chest puffed out proudly.

But he'd be well advised never to forget what shaped and forged him: my Milan. It was thanks to the Scudetto won by that team that Allegri was able to become an attractive recruit for the major clubs. He'd shown that he knew how to win, and now everyone knew it. Even if he was no tactical genius, Max was especially skilful at managing the dressing room, being both intelligent and politically shrewd.

But there was one thing he did that I could never really swallow: his rejection of the offer from Real Madrid. I know it was a concrete offer. Why did he take the safer option in Italy, instead of going out and accepting the challenge? This kind of refusal also tells the world what sort of person you are.

You muster your courage, you go where you're wanted, you try it out and see what it's like to work in a foreign country, where everything is harder; you walk on fire, and you do what Ancelotti did – a man who won everywhere and who never stopped growing, thanks to his wealth of new experiences.

I could have stayed a lot longer at Ajax, and the same goes for Juve, but instead I chose to take on all the challenges, in order to become the best. The only team I played for in Sweden was the youth team. After that I always played outside Sweden, in other people's back yards, where things are so much harder for a foreigner.

Instead, though, Allegri made the simplest choice, the least risky one, and stayed in Italy.

It would have been nice if Antonio Conte, too, had remained in Italy and taken up the challenge of trying to win again, with a weaker Inter. The stature and grandeur of a battle are determined not by the outcome, but by the courage you show in fighting it. Someone like Conte can't simply fall back on becoming a football pundit on television; it's a pleasure to see him in the dugout at Tottenham once more.

Too bad. Serie A would have been even more spectacular with Conte and Gattuso; Mourinho, Sarri, Allegri, Spalletti and Pioli. Just think of the battles.

4. The Ball
(or About Love)

The most wonderful football of my life was the Select ball we played with as children in Malmö. It was made of rubber and it was spangled with stars. The more it bounced and skidded on dirt and gravel, the mangier it became – and the more perfect it became. Because it wasn't right when it was new, clean and shiny. What with all the kicks it took and all the rocks it skidded across, the Select shed its skin like a snake, bits and pieces came off it, it lost its scales and turned into a white patch, a cloud in the dust. And, all things considered, that was what made it perfect.

I never loved a football again the way I loved that patchy, mangy Select of Rosengård. It was the bright sun of our neighbourhood. We all orbited around it, from dawn to dusk. I felt as if I could do anything with that ball. I dreamed up feints, dribbles, tricks, challenges, dares and battles . . . It was with that ball at my feet that I began to dream.

I can't stand listening to players talk about how they first started playing with a football made of rags or old socks, and that they would dribble stones, coconuts or tin cans. As if they were all so many Pelés. Bullshit! Most of them do it to transform their life stories into fairy tales. What's the point?

My ball of rags was that mangy old Select. It took me a while to understand the importance of holding on to the meaningful objects of my career. At the beginning I kept nothing. I don't even own any of my old shirts from Ajax and Juventus.

I thought only about the future, about running forward, not looking back. Then it finally dawned on me one day that it would be nice to tell my sons about the path I had pursued, and old objects would surely be a help in doing that. When you can touch them – the actual objects – you remember more clearly. Since that day I've been keeping everything: shirts, boots, footballs.

For now I keep them in plastic bags, because Helena doesn't like seeing them on display around the house. Neither do I, truth be told, but one day I'll build myself a museum. And in that museum the adidas football with its thin stripes from the bicycle kick against England will enjoy pride of place.

I've kept all the footballs from my hat-tricks, with the autographs of the other players on them, which, according to tradition, I was allowed to take home. Another ball that wound up in a plastic bag is the one with which I scored the goal against Italy in the 2004 UEFA European Championship: a Roteiro. That wasn't a hat-trick, so by rights I shouldn't have been allowed to keep it. I sent a friend of mine, who happens to be an executive on the national team, out on a mission to get it. I told him, 'You absolutely need to lay your hands on it.'

He was successful. And now I have it at home.

To me, a football isn't just a work tool; it's not a computer that I leave in the office when I go home. It's an object of love – it's a part of me, a living thing, like a dog that wanders around the house and which every so often I lovingly pet, pick up and put back down. We have footballs in every room of the house. When I come across one, I take it out for a short walk, I move it along with my feet, I dribble it a time or two, try out a feint and then leave it there.

If I happen to see Maxi or Vincent in the same room I'll try and dribble past them and – who knows – maybe we might play a lightning-quick game. Which sends Helena into a rage. She doesn't like it when we get underfoot in the kitchen.

My sons have learned from me. They'll get on a video call from Stockholm and I can see, even in Milan, that while they're looking at me on the screen and talking to me, they're dribbling a football. If you live like that, the ball becomes part of you. You no longer think of it as something outside you. It's no longer like a shoe; it becomes like your foot.

I've heard that a Brazilian journalist once sighed, as he watched Pelé running down the pitch with the ball seemingly glued to his foot, 'I wish I had the kind of intimacy with my wife that Pelé has with the ball.'

I've always had that intimacy with the ball. It was the other kind of intimacy that I had more problems with.

When I was a young man I was too in love with myself and I had a raging ego, which prevented me from taking any real interest in another person. I wondered if I'd ever be capable of loving someone.

Plus, I was very shy. I trembled every time I talked to a

girl. I was always extremely nervous. That's why I did everything quite late, when compared to my group of friends. When I went out on my first date I jotted down notes on everything I would have to say. If she gave an unexpected answer or presented a new topic, I'd go on anyway with the next question on my scrap of paper. It wasn't exactly a simple conversation.

I lived in a middle ground between two very distant worlds. When I played football, on the other hand, I felt I was the strongest player and I was afraid of nothing. Off the pitch, however, I was riddled with insecurities.

In my head, the first thing for me was the football – not girls, like so many of my friends, who never thought of anything else, boasting constantly of their conquests and their escapades. I liked to go to the clubs and meet girls as much as anyone else, but I didn't want to talk about them or, above all, have a steady girlfriend.

I've only had two relationships in my whole life: one before Helena, and then Helena herself.

But the only real relationship that mattered to me when I was a young man was with the football.

To foreigners, Swedish girls are all beautiful, blonde, smiling, emancipated and uninhibited. I first discovered that world of the imagination when I was seventeen years old and I ventured into the centre of Malmö for the first time. In the neighbourhood where I lived we were all foreigners, the girls had dark eyes and dark hair and many of them wore a veil. And when I got to Stockholm, they were even more stunning and daunting. I thought to myself: 'All these blondes in the same square . . . It's just not normal.'

As I grew up, the two worlds drew closer and closer together.

The strength that I drew from football and my first successes was making me more and more self-confident off the pitch as well. I no longer had to act, to seem different from how I really was. Now I'd say to myself: 'You're fine, Zlatan, you're okay the way you are. If she doesn't like you, that's her problem.'

When I first got to Amsterdam to play for Ajax, I went to tour the 'red-light district': the canals, the ladies of the night looking out of their windows, and so forth. I was curious – I'd heard so much about the place. My friends from Malmö would come and visit me and ask me to take them for a tour of the district, and it was all okay until the day I heard someone exclaim, 'It's Ibrahimović!'

I'd been recognized. Since that day I haven't set foot there again. If my employers at Ajax had spotted me in the red-light district, they'd have killed me.

There's something Vujadin Boškov used to say that's become notorious: 'If a man chooses his woman over a cold beer and the Champions League final, it may be true love, but he's not a true man.'

No, that makes him a true man.

In any love story, the sex at the beginning is pure adrenaline, then it becomes something even more important because it binds the couple together, helps them to grow in intimacy and makes that experience unique.

In a certain sense, football nurtures the relationship between me and Helena because it separates us, sending me out with my team for away games, shutting us up in a hotel, and therefore it strengthens our desire.

Helena isn't jealous. She's more mature than that, she has more experience. She knew me when I was just a boy, and she knows that I was shy, that I wasn't a girl-chaser. She knows what I'm like. She knows that I'm doing fine. And that if you're happy with someone, there's no need for you to go in search of anything else. She trusts me. And I trust her. I'm not the kind of guy who's going to go and check his significant other's mobile phone. When I was younger, I guess, maybe I would have done, but our relationship is a solid one, based on deep trust and mutual respect. Without those two pillars, no relationship can function for twenty years.

A while ago I was in Sardinia, so I stopped by to say hello to Silvio Berlusconi in his villa. We kidded around about more or less everything, even about love.

I've always enjoyed spending time with the team president, even though he invariably asks me to get my hair cut. Whenever Berlusconi arrived in Milanello, there was no need to actually lay eyes on him. You could sense it in the air and, when he walked into a room, everyone there would straighten their back, sit up or stand straight and apparently stop breathing entirely. I admire people who emanate this aura of power, who instil respect in you and perhaps even a hint of fear.

I remember the evening I was presented to the fans at the San Siro Stadium, before the Milan–Lecce match in 2010. I walk down onto the pitch, I wave to the audience in my new shirt, then I climb up into the stand to watch the match. Berlusconi gets me to take a seat next to him and Adriano Galliani.

We watch the first half and then, just as the second half is starting, the team president turns to me and asks, 'Ibra, would you mind moving over one seat? A very important person is arriving.'

'Why of course. It's no problem.'

I move over, and so does Galliani. I'm expecting a politician or a ranking executive from some other major club.

Ten minutes go by, but no one shows up. The seat remains empty.

After fifteen minutes or so, everyone stands up and a beautiful woman walks in, on dizzyingly high heels. She takes her seat.

Berlusconi leans over and gives me a wink: 'A very important person . . .'

I love my sons more than anything else on Earth. As far as I'm concerned, they're always in pole position.

Loving them also means protecting them and responsibly managing their freedom. They're not allowed to spend time on social-media platforms, because I don't want them to be hurt by the nasty comments they might read about me. On my Instagram account there's not a single photo of my sons or my family.

What I do see, though, is lots of children putting all sorts onto the internet; some of them have parents who have created a personal account for them on social media and, while they're still only seven or eight years old, they can already boast thousands of followers. But when those children grow up, are they going to be happy that they were exposed to all those eyes in that fashion? What do their parents really know about what's good for them? My children are going to be able to make their own decisions, but only once they're capable of understanding the kinds of lies and hypocrisy you encounter in the world of internet platforms. They can't possibly know it now – so no social media for them.

I'm not talking about trying to keep them under a bell jar. It's my responsibility to blaze a path for them. They'll be free to pursue that path as they see best, as soon as they're ready to walk on their own two feet. And if they're still living under my roof when they're twenty-five, that will mean that maybe I got it wrong somehow.

Maxi and Vincent have also had to learn to read between the lines when it comes to their friendships. They're good at it: 'Why does this person want to be my friend?' They've come to distance themselves from certain friends who hung around with them only because I'm their father. Their decision, not mine.

I'll never forget that, when I was their age, my teammates' parents circulated a petition to expel me from the group because they considered me to be a bully. I don't expel anyone from any groups. I'm only careful to make sure that my celebrity and popularity have no negative repercussions on my sons.

I've said it before: at first Maxi and Vincent hated football. They were jealous of it but, now that they've entered my world, I'm no longer just a father to them; I'm also their coach, and they listen to me in a very different way. The problem, though, is that I'm very direct: if someone fails to give their all, as they're supposed to, I speak to that person in exactly the same way, whether they are Brahim Díaz or one of my sons. If I have to say it, then I go right ahead and say it: 'You weren't working very hard today; you were so lazy it was disgusting.'

I don't know how to communicate more diplomatically than that because, according to my philosophy, I'm not really working in someone's best interests if I fail to tell them the way things really are.

The same goes on the pitch. If I criticize a teammate and point out, 'Look, you made a mistake there', then that teammate, who might have been convinced he did the right thing, will reflect and the next time he won't make the same mistake.

When I go to my sons' training sessions I never take selfies or pictures with the other people, because in the stand I'm merely a father – I'm not Ibra. That's my boys' space, and *they* need to be important there; *I* don't. They are Maximilian and Vincent, not Zlatan's sons. That's why we enrolled them at school under my wife's surname. They shouldn't have to go through life being the sons of Ibrahimović.

I have talked to them about it: 'Boys, you're going to need to be much stronger mentally than I was at your age. At school, on the pitch, everywhere you go, you're going to have to deal with being compared to me. There's no escaping it. If you aren't strong and resilient in your minds, it's going to be too hard for you. It's not your fault and it's not my fault. That's just the way it is.'

My eldest, Maximilian, has a solid personality. At a certain point I decided that the time had come to ask him, 'What name do you want to use? Seger or Ibrahimović? You can choose.' My wife's surname will ensure him greater protection, more freedom; mine will force him to face conflict head-on, every time.

Maximilian replied, 'I'm an Ibrahimović.'

He feels sure of his decision, but Vincent still has to choose. It's too soon for him. He's only one year younger, but at that age, a year counts for a lot.

I manage to watch the boys' training sessions and their matches from Milan, thanks to a video camera set up on the pitch at Hammarby in Stockholm. That enables me to keep an eye on how things are going. Then I talk to them directly, we discuss things and we compare impressions and ideas.

One day I saw Vincent being comforted by his coach. Something must have happened. After the training session, I call the little one over and tell him, 'As soon as you're alone, in your room, ring me.'

When Vincent phones, I ask, 'How are you?' It's a video call. I immediately notice that he's avoiding looking into the screen and that he's short of breath. I tell him, 'Relax, Vincent. Take a deep breath and, when you feel ready, tell me how you are.'

He calms down and, after a few minutes, he answers me: 'I'm not okay.'

I understand that this is taking effort, and that it's not easy for him to admit what's wrong. Both boys always want to seem strong when they're talking to me. They don't need to prove anything to me, but in their minds they feel they must, especially since they've started devoting themselves to football with great passion.

They go to Helena and ask her constantly, 'What does Papa think of me?' They want to be perfect in my eyes. They can't understand that, as far as I'm concerned, they're already perfect the way they are, simply because they're alive in this world; and all the more so, if they're happy.

That said, I have to admit that I do have my own quite direct way of saying things and I definitely tend to apply pressure. I always tell them, 'Why do you want to be ordinary, if you can be the best instead? But that's up to you – it's your choice. You're free to live your own life.'

I never want to be ordinary, because there are lots of ordinary people out there, and only a few people are the best. That's why I always give 200 per cent at everything I try to do.

'I'm not okay,' Vincent tells me.

'What's wrong?' I ask him.

'I miss you.'

He might as well have plunged a knife into my heart and twisted it. 'I'm going to rip up my contract with Milan right now and turn around and go home,' I think to myself, 'because my sons come first. There's nothing more important to me in this world.'

Vincent has always been close to me; he's always felt protected. This is the first time we've been separated, but I only expected to stay at Milan for six months. If I'd known my contract was going to be extended, I would have kept my family with me. In part, I'm forced to admit, it was a good thing, because it helped me to loosen the pressure I was exerting on my sons.

I'll never say to them, 'You have to become professional footballers.' No, never. But I do say, 'If you have a chance to become one, and if you really want it to happen, then give it your all, at every match, at every training session, and do your best to succeed.'

When we were in Los Angeles I'd drive three hours to take Maxi and Vincent to the pitch where their team played, and then go and pick them up. I made things very clear to them. 'Boys, I don't have any time to waste. I'll only take you if you're willing to give it everything you've got.'

The same thing went for Taekwondo, and they both became black belts.

'I'll only take you to the gym if you're willing to give two hundred per cent. Otherwise, it's pointless to waste time. Stay at home and read books.'

That applies to everything, not only sports. Are you good at it? Not good at it? I don't care. But if you're going to do it for an hour or two, then you have to give it your all – everything you've got inside you. That's my philosophy.

And it's the same philosophy I adopt at Milan.

If you do just enough in training and you face off against me half-heartedly, then you're not doing me a favour. In fact you're simply interfering with my training, because you're not helping me to improve.

You need to give it your all, because if you do, then I'm forced to give it my all as well. You improve *me* and I improve *you*. If you're doing a shitty job of training, then you might as well go home, because you're undermining yourself and other people. That's how I changed the mindset at Milan.

Still, every now and then I find myself in an awkward situation, because I realize that I'm not treating Maxi and Vincent as sons, but as footballers. Helena warns me, 'Look out, because you need to give them love, too.'

She's right: they need balance, equilibrium. She knows it because, when Maxi and Vincent are unhappy, they confide in her, while with me they always want to come off strong, to be like me.

'Papa, I miss you.'

At first, when Vincent said that to me, I wanted to rush right home, because after all I don't have anything left to prove on the pitch. I'm here to give, not to take. I'm here to help. I've done so much in my career that now I'm strictly interested in inspiring others and helping them to become stronger.

But football is my passion, it's my life. Without football, I'm just an empty shell.

I've already mentioned how terrified I am at the thought of leaving a thoroughly programmed life and going back into regular, everyday life, with no idea of what to do, and with no control over my own future. And that's why I extended my contract with Milan for another year, without even discussing it with Helena.

She didn't lose her temper, but she did tell me, 'You should have talked it over with me first. You'll live in Italy and we'll live in Sweden, so we need to get organized to see each other regularly and take care of the practical aspects.'

I know it was selfish of me, and the only consideration I had was my own fear of retirement. I pushed into the future the moment of saying goodbye, because I'm so scared of it. I ought to have talked it over with Helena, so that we could put our heads together and consider all the various options: quitting entirely, going back to Sweden, continuing with Milan or transferring somewhere else.

Instead I thought only about football and the way it pumps up my blood and sends adrenaline coursing through my veins, filling my lungs with oxygen, making me feel fully alive. I thought about the 80,000 fans who would come back to the San Siro, my home stadium, and make me feel like a lion in the arena.

But when your own son tells you, 'Papa, I miss you', the whole castle crumbles to dust and even a guy like me turns back into an ordinary father. Vincent killed me with that 'I miss you.'

And so I told Helena, 'All of you, come straight down here.' They landed at Linate Airport the following morning.

The first thing Vincent said was, 'Let's go and see Papa.'

Helena rightly explained to him, 'He's training at Milanello, and that's far away from here. We'll wait for him at home. He'll be there in the early afternoon.'

But Vincent wasn't willing to wait. He pressured Helena into taking a taxi and they all came out to Milanello. We stayed together for a few days, and then Maximilian left for Trentino with the AC Milan Academy, because he's happy to spend time with me, but he may be even happier when he can play football. By now he's entered my world.

I suggested to him, 'Go and have a ten-day retreat, and you'll get a taste of the life I live: training, hotel, et cetera. You'll meet new teammates. And you'll like it in the mountains.'

Vincent stayed with me in Milan and we replenished our stores of energy, then he went back to Sweden with his mother. He landed at five in the afternoon at Stockholm and immediately insisted on going to training.

Helena pointed out to him, 'Training starts at five-thirty. We can't get there in time.'

'Let's try, at least,' Vincent insisted.

'By the time we swing by the house and you get to the ground, they'll already have finished.'

'I don't care, I'm happy to have even five minutes of training.'

Helena gave in and took him to the pitch. Now Vincent, too, has entered my world.

When Helena came back to pick up Maxi, Vincent didn't come because that weekend he had a match. He misses me, but football is a powerful passion that makes up for it. And I'm happy, because my sons didn't grow up unbridled, the way I did in Malmö, where I went out whenever I pleased and went to play football in the Rose Garden. Instead, ever since they were small, they've been watched over and protected but then, as they grew, little by little, they've earned more and more freedom. Football helps them to have teammates and friends, to live according to the values and relations of the dressing room.

They both play for Hammarby Fotboll. They didn't make the team because they're Ibrahimović's sons. They were both obliged to compete for admission, like all the others, under my wife's surname.

I was nowhere in sight. The club accepted my sons because of what they showed they could do in the two-week trial, not because of me. They have teammates from every neighbourhood in town that they're friends with. That's their home now: the dressing room.

Vincent is very intelligent on the pitch. I don't say that because he's my son. His coaches were extremely impressed the minute they saw him play. 'He plays like a grown man. He's much more mature than you'd expect from his age. Really, way ahead . . .' It's the truth.

If I ask him, 'How did it go in training?' he'll reply, 'Really well, Papa, today I didn't miss a single ball.' He doesn't say what I always used to say: 'Really great. I scored a goal, I did a spectacular piece of dribbling and a bicycle kick.' No.

'I didn't miss a single ball.' At his age, I wanted the same thing that every other kid of my age wanted. I wanted to astonish my friends and prove that I was a better player than anyone else. I'd invent feints, magical moves, circus acts with my mangy old Select football.

Vincent is a spider at the centre of the web, weaving the play of the whole team. He's a number six – he keeps the ball moving. He's not looking for the most sensational pass; he just wants the simplest one, which is almost always the most useful one. If he scores a goal he's happy about it, but if he can provide an assist for a teammate to score that goal, he's much happier still. His coach has a point: Vincent plays like a man.

Maximilian also plays midfield, but he sees his role differently. With the physique and power that he has, he can outrun all the others from one penalty area to the other. One day he'll feel like Ronaldinho and push forward; another day he'll feel like Paul Pogba and fall back. He has yet to figure out exactly what his true position is.

Helena is mainly in charge of school. At most, I help the boys with mathematics because I've always been fascinated by numbers. And ever since someone scammed me in Malmö, numbers have become even more important to me.

I've always enjoyed solving problems in my head, or counting on my fingers, without writing on paper. At school I always came up with the right solution, but then I didn't know how to show my work, or prove how I'd come to that answer. I taught my sons how to solve problems in their heads and count on their fingers.

Helena takes care of everything else and then reports back to me, because she understands that I want to know everything about Maxi and Vincent. If something serious happens, then I'll weigh in. But I've never caused an uproar over a bad grade. After all, neither Einstein nor I really wowed at school.

I've never laid a finger on my children to punish them. I took regular beatings from my mother, but those were different times and we lived in a different situation: she was a mother of five with lots of problems at home, struggling in the relentlessly stressful situation of poverty.

At any rate, all the times she banged me over the head with a wooden spoon did nothing to keep me from growing up happy, and achieving success.

Back then it was a normal thing to get a beating from your parents.

To me, discipline is immensely important. It's right for my sons to respect me, without fearing me, but they also need to know exactly what will happen if they make a mistake. I don't want to have to repeat fifty times, 'That's not right, that's not right . . .' If I say it once, that needs to be enough.

This goes for training, too, where I expect them to give their all: heart and soul. One example: I take my family up into the mountains, for a nineteen-mile trek. Me and the boys on mountain bikes, Helena on the electric bike. The climb is hard and challenging, even for me and Maxi. After two and a half miles, Vincent is aching in his back and his abdominals, but he doesn't want to give up. According to my mindset, he needs to keep going, because this is the age when you learn to clench your teeth and refuse to surrender.

'Slow down – stop and get off. Walk a little . . .' No, that's not the way I am. I say: 'Keep going and learn to suffer.' That's how things are in my world.

When I went back to working out, after the operation on my knee, I suffered all day long, but that never bothered me because I'm used to it. I've suffered all my life, one way or another. In fact not only does it not bother me, I actually enjoy it to a certain extent. When I go through a difficult and painful situation, I suffer and I enjoy it.

But Vincent was really struggling, so Helena insisted on letting him use her electric bike. She took the mountain bike, and we all went back down to the bottom of the mountain, without stopping.

The next day we hiked uphill, and at a certain point the boys took off at a run because they claimed I wasn't going fast enough. Maybe they wanted to show me how strong they were or perhaps, more simply, they were looking for a challenge. By now they need it, just like I do.

In fact they train on their own in the gym at our house, in Stockholm. They call me up and ask me for the right programmes to work out with, on the treadmill.

One day, while I was still rehabilitating, Vincent came to Milanello with me. While I was doing my exercises, he told me, 'Papa, I want to do some running on the pitch.'

'Okay, do thirty sprints, box to box.'

The AC Milan coaches turned to watch. 'What's he doing? That's not normal.'

'He's training,' I explained.

'Sure, but not even the players in the first team work like that.'

Then Pioli showed up, too. 'This is self-discipline. I think I know who taught it to him.'

'Coach, I don't tiptoe around when I'm talking to anyone. Whether it's Vincent, Maxi or Theo Hernández – if there's work to be done, then I expect hard work.'

Then we're in Ibiza. I do my training and I go back to the boat. It's noon.

I ask Helena, 'Where are the boys?'

They're still sleeping. At noon.

I alert the captain. 'Halt the engines, we're not going out to sea.' I wake up Maxi and Vincent. 'Put on your trainers and let's go work out. You have two minutes to get ready.'

They leave the boat with sleep still in their eyes. They haven't even had a chance to brush their teeth. I find a road where we can do sprints back and forth. I count out the metres and mark the start and finish lines on the pavement.

'Every time I give you the signal, start sprinting.'

They break into a run. Maxi, who's bigger and stronger, sprints back and forth without difficulty. The younger boy, who of course can't keep pace with his brother, pushes his face into my chest and says, 'Papa, I can't go on.'

I count down: 'Three, two, one . . .'

Vincent breaks into a run again. He reaches the far end of the distance. He folds over, both hands on his knees. He takes off into the final sprint.

I tell him, 'Good work, Vincent. Let's go.'

No hugs, no kisses – nothing of the sort. Nothing but 'Good work'.

Now Vincent knows that, even if he thinks he's a wreck, he can still complete the task he's set out to do. Now he knows that unless you walk on fire, you'll never find that out.

5. The Agent
(or About Wealth)

It's true that I offered my services to Paris Saint-Germain in summer 2021, but not as a footballer. No, it was as a sports director. I called club president Nasser Al-Khelaïfi and suggested the following: 'If I don't extend my contract with Milan, I'll come to PSG and fix your team for you.'

Nasser laughed, but he didn't say no.

Mino Raiola agreed, too. He told me, 'That's your position. Go on and take it. Period.'

Mino knew perfectly well that by now there was an unbreakable bond between me and Milan – a special chemistry. Even if I'd received offers from Real Madrid or Barcelona, my answer would have been 'No, Mino. I'm really happy here at Milan. And if I'm happy somewhere, then I feel no need to make any changes.'

I've said it before: I have nothing that I'm trying to prove. I only want to give back what I was given. Give some portion of myself to the young players, help them to grow in such a way that one day they'll be able to take Milan even further into the future.

Raiola was well aware that he'd never be able to prise me free of Milan, but he still agreed with me: if I decided not to extend my stay there, then the role of director at Paris Saint-Germain would be the right next move.

All the PSG players that I talked to agreed.

One of them told me, 'Zlatan, only you can fix this team and bring discipline back.'

Another said, 'Zlatan, if you'd been here, this thing in the dressing room wouldn't have happened.'

I liked the project, but it wasn't enough to help me get over the sensation of sheer panic and fear that washed over me at the thought of ending my career as a player. It's one thing to say it, quite another matter to actually do it. I'd go to Paris, I'd take one look at team training and I'd ask myself a thousand times: 'Why did you ever quit?'

And so, when all was said and done, I extended my contract with AC Milan. But if some day a concrete opportunity comes along, maybe it will be less difficult for me to quit, even if I already know now that there's no other position I could hope for that will ever give me the adrenaline surge I get from playing on the pitch. Mino has already announced it to the world: 'Zlatan's future is as an executive.'

Anyway, this is the truth: I didn't offer myself to Paris Saint-Germain as a player, but as a sports director.

After that, Nasser really lost his temper with me. He called me up and told me, 'Zlatan, I can't believe that you advised Kylian Mbappé to transfer to Real Madrid.'

I could have denied it, I could have sworn to him that someone had lied to him, but instead I gave it to him straight. 'It's the truth, Nasser. I did.'

'Why?' he asked me.

'Because there's not enough discipline at PSG, and discipline is what Mbappé needs in order to improve, grow and take his next step. It's impossible now in Paris, because you don't have the right people.'

If there were more rigorous leadership, everyone would be running on the pitch, no one would show up late for training, nor would they even dream of doing as they please.

If I were there, I wouldn't ask people to do things: I'd *tell* them to do them. I don't have anything personal against Leonardo Araújo. In fact I like him. He was the one who brought me to PSG, and there's not a single thing I can criticize him for. Still, I know the difference between him and me. I don't ask; I order.

PSG changed its history in forty-eight hours: from an ordinary club, it transformed itself to its present-day dimension. If you don't have a strong executive, with all the stars you've signed, the team becomes unmanageable.

Let me sum up PSG for you.

Do they pay their salaries? Yes.

Do they win the championship? Yes.

Is life pleasant in Paris? Yes.

There are forty players, but no one wants to leave, even if they don't get a chance to play, because life is just too good there.

If I were in charge, everyone would spend their days on the rack, being tormented. Because if I give you a pay cheque and you fail to give me your all in exchange, then you can hit the road. That's what I call discipline.

My advice to Mbappé: 'Try to get out of there.'

My advice to Nasser: 'Try to keep him from leaving.'

Two pieces of honest advice. I told them exactly what I thought, the way I always do.

I met Kylian Mbappé at Marco Verratti's wedding and he asked me, 'In your opinion, Zlatan, what should I do?'

'Well, the way I see it, you need to go to Real Madrid, to get to know a club that has a different philosophy and different rules of the game.'

You learn your values from your surroundings, from the champions you work alongside. At PSG there are lots of stars, but not a lot of sacrifice, because there's no need. They use just half of their potential; after all, they win all the same. If the top of the pyramid is weak, then the base will be, too.

If a player receives an order, he says, 'Okay, will do.' Then he complains to Nasser, who agrees with him, and the sports director discovers he's been given the runaround.

But if I'm that sports director, and that player tries to pull a fast one like that on me, it's going to be the last thing he does. I guarantee it.

Let me tell you how I arrived in Paris. As a player.

Summer 2012: I meet with Galliani at headquarters, we chat and I confirm, 'I'm happy here in Milan. I'm not moving.' Then I give Mino an order: 'Don't call me while I'm on holiday. Let me be. Forget you even have my phone number.' Because if an agent or a sports director calls you up, it's never to ask how your holidays are proceeding. It's only ever to suggest a transfer, and I'd already decided I wouldn't be leaving Milan, because I was happy where I was.

After three weeks on holiday I return home from a

fishing trip on a Swedish lake and I turn on my mobile. Six calls from Mino, all unanswered.

Helena tells me, 'Mino's trying to get in touch with me.'

He called her, too. So there's something on the boil . . . But I don't call him back. I don't want to leave. I'm happy at Milan.

I was still smarting from my experience with Barcelona, where I'd gone in pursuit of a dream and that dream was destroying me. It's true that I've always needed to change clubs, but this time the grass of Milan seemed greener than anywhere else.

Mino, who charges like a buffalo when he wants something, calls me for a whole day and, in the end, I'm forced to answer: 'I told you not to call me.'

'I wanted to know how you were doing,' he replies.

'Forget about how I'm doing. Don't call me again, because I know what you want.' I didn't have the faintest idea what club he might have in mind. I just wasn't interested.

'I'm coming to Sweden.' There's Mino on the attack.

'Why?'

'Because I need to talk to you.'

'But I'm not *in* Sweden.'

'Oh yes, you are. I'll be landing this afternoon and then we'll get together.'

'All right.'

I settle down to wait for him.

Mino shows up with his lawyers and starts talking. 'Your future is no longer Milan. Call Galliani and check it out for yourself: they don't even have enough money to meet the payroll any more. Your future is now called Paris Saint-Germain.'

'PSG?'

'PSG.'

The club had already made some signings: Thiago Motta, Maxwell, Javier Pastore . . . In a flash, I envision the transfer: me wearing the PSG shirt, in a small stadium somewhere out in the sticks, in the French league. I imagine myself, I see myself, and I listen to myself, to see if I start to feel a little adrenaline surge into my veins. Nope, not even a drop.

'No, I'm not going to Paris.'

At that very moment Leonardo calls. 'Zlatan, Paris is just waiting for you.'

'Listen, Leonardo, I want to talk to you with the utmost honesty and transparency: I seriously don't see myself playing an away game, in some backwater country stadium, in front of a crowd of 2,000. That's not my style. I'm used to playing for 80,000 fans who may love me or may hate me but, whichever is the case, certainly pump me up with energy and excitement. Don't take this the wrong way, but your offer does nothing to excite me.'

In response, Leonardo reacted very well, because he did nothing to try to question the obvious facts, but instead spoke straight from the heart. 'You're right. That's exactly the case, and there's nothing I can do about it. You're going to have to get used to small stadiums. But let me assure you, PSG is the future and, with the investments that we're going to make, we'll build a very different world, and we'll take on the most prestigious clubs in all of Europe.'

I hang up.

I'm not convinced. They insist, and I continue to resist. But when Mino gets something into his head, there's no stopping him. He simply keeps rolling forward like a panzer tank. Plus, he's way too intelligent – he always knows how to construct the right sentences. If you don't know him well, you can't appreciate it, but it's true. He didn't tell me, 'PSG is loaded with cash.' No, he started talking to me about the future: programmes, investments, visions, and players they want to buy. In the end he asks me, 'How much do you want?'

Usually a contract includes the salary and a few other bonuses: a house, a certain number of trips home, that kind of thing.

I think it over for a while and then I reply, 'I want this much money, and then I want this, that and also this . . .' I ask for everything that pops into my head. Mino jots down notes on a sheet of paper and, by the time he's done, he's written out a full page crammed with bonuses.

My strategy is clear: shoot for the moon, demanding so much that they'll have to tell *me* no, and I won't have to say no to *them*.

'Don't you want a nice bicycle, so you can take a little ride around the centre of town?' Mino asks me mockingly, after that machine-gun burst of requests.

'Good thinking! Let's throw in a bicycle.'

He keeps his cool. 'I'll report back to Leonardo and I'll let you know.'

I felt absolutely relaxed.

But then, just twenty minutes later, Mino announces, 'Leonardo has accepted all your terms. Even the bicycle.'

At that point I had to go to Paris. I'd given my word, and my word is worth more than a signed contract.

I look at Mino for one final confirmation. 'So it's decided? We're going to Paris? Are you really sure? We're doing this?'

Mino replies, 'Zlatan, we don't have any choice in the matter. Milan has already sold you.'

'What do you mean, they've sold me?'

'Berlusconi and Galliani have gift-wrapped you, along with Thiago Silva. They've tied the bow, set the price and all the rest.'

At last the scales fall from my eyes. 'Draft the contract: we're leaving.'

While I was battling to stay on at Milan, Milan had already dumped me in France, without bothering to tell me. My meeting with Galliani had been a farce, as had been his promise to keep me.

'It's all okay.' I didn't speak to Galliani for months.

At first only one of us was supposed to leave, either me or Silva, and the other would be transferred to Paris the following season, and then they decided to package us up together. Berlusconi justified his decision as follows: 'I'd rather eat shit only once, instead of twice.'

I get to Paris Saint-Germain and I find sheer hell. Don't think of the rich and well-organized top club it is today.

First of all, some guy hands me a big gym bag and

explains, 'This is your kit for the whole season. You'll have to bring it with you every time you come to the pitch.'

'My friend, we need to get a few things straight,' I retort. 'I'm not carrying anything anywhere. You are the ones who are going to have to make sure that, at every match and every training session, I find my kit ready and sweet-smelling in the dressing room, washed, dried and ironed.'

There were three kitmen and three physios for twenty-five players. The training pitches were a disaster. Sometimes the grass was in such miserable condition that we had to play on synthetic turf.

The cook asks me, 'What do you want tomorrow, meat or seafood?'

'I don't know, I'll tell you tomorrow.'

'No, you need to let us know now. That way we can start cooking tomorrow's meal this evening.'

I look at him in surprise. 'I expect fresh food. If you don't do your best job of making dinner, I can't do my best job of playing and winning. Understood?'

After playing for a highly organized club like Milan, this was something of a nightmare. Players at PSG today can't begin to imagine what it was like at the start.

I even had problems finding somewhere good to live. The places were either too small or they just wouldn't do. At first we lived in a *hôtel particulier*. It was a very luxurious and expensive town house, but that was PSG's problem, not mine. My choice of housing had been one of the conditions that I'd insisted on in my contract. Also living in that *hôtel particulier* were Kim Kardashian and Kanye

West. Every time I went out the front door I found myself face-to-face with forty paparazzi and, believe me, I didn't love it.

Then we moved to an apartment near the Champs-Élysées, but it was a noisy neighbourhood, busy with traffic. After eight at night, all hell broke loose.

In the end I found a newly renovated building, near the Arc de Triomphe, not far from avenue Victor Hugo, in a nice, quiet neighbourhood, and we were very happy living there. They gave me three apartments: one for me, one for guests and one for Dario, my physio, whom I'd met in Milan and who by now was a member of my family – so much so that he always spent his Christmas holidays with us in Sweden.

I had Italian teammates, such as Verratti and Salvatore Sirigu, and others who had played in Serie A, such as Pastore, Silva and Ezequiel Lavezzi, which meant we did a lot of talking in Italian, even if that did annoy the French players.

I have to admit that Leonardo Araújo was brilliant. In just one year he built a team that played excellently, a group that struck fear into the hearts of others. My last thought before leaving Paris, after four years there, was this: 'Some day this team will win the Champions League. They won't stop until they've brought the trophy home.'

What sealed my farewell was the quarter-final match against Manchester City in 2016, in my last season. It was no ordinary game. To make this perfectly clear, club president Nasser came in person expressly to tell us this in the dressing room before the match in Paris. It was basically a family derby, a final reckoning between emirs and sheikhs – the United Arab Emirates, as the owner of Manchester City, against Qatar, as the owner of PSG – a battle between superpowers.

So I step onto the pitch and almost immediately screw up a penalty and then, with the score still 0–0, I also miss an easy goal on a pass from Thiago Motta. I score to make it 1–1 and then, when it's 2–1, I hit the crossbar: that ball could have sealed the match.

The final score is 2–2. In the second leg, a goal by Kevin De Bruyne eliminates us. Mino, who's considerably more far-sighted than I am, tells me directly after the Paris match, 'We're done here. It's time to leave. They're not going to extend your contract.'

And I reply, 'What are you talking about? I'm on excellent terms with him. I'll talk to the president and everything will be fine. Wait and see. Stop worrying.'

I meet Nasser and he's using all these strange turns of phrase and brings up one weak excuse after another: you've been here for four years; four years is such a long time, blah-blah-blah.

I stop him. 'President, let's not beat about the bush. It's either yes or no.'

So he proceeds to explain, 'We're trying to build a new generation of players. We need to rejuvenate the team.'

Mino had understood everything before it happened, as always. Maybe there was an overarching plan that would have come into effect in any case, whatever the result of the match, but I'm still convinced that the fluffed penalty against City changed the outcome.

There I am, without a contract. I didn't know which way to turn. Then it happens, all at once. Mourinho goes to Manchester United and reaches out to me: 'Come play for me.'

Except that the situation is very confusing. José signs, but then he has a fight with the club. My contract keeps going back and forth and nothing gets resolved. They tell me to wait a couple of days, and then I go to Monte Carlo with Mino. The plan is to leave Monte Carlo for Manchester. But after a week we haven't heard a word from anyone.

'Mino, enough is enough,' I say. 'I'm sick of this whole thing.'

Mino replies, 'Be patient. You just need to be patient, Zlatan.' Sure, no doubt: be patient. How am I supposed to do that?

In fact I go on Instagram and write, 'My next club will be Manchester United.' I am so caught up in the negotiations that it never even occurs to me that Man U is a publicly traded company. You can't make that kind of an announcement if there's no official, signed agreement. All hell breaks loose in half the world's capitals.

Mino is ready to kill me. 'Zlatan, you fucked up big time.'

I can't take any more of that situation. I can't stand being stalled, so I decide to venture a move and try to prompt a reaction: either in or out.

Ed Woodward, executive vice-chairman of Manchester United, is furious.

I try to explain, I apologize, 'This was entirely my fault.

My agent, Mino Raiola, had nothing to do with it. I got impatient, that's all. I felt like I was caught in quicksand, I was going under and I tried to do something to get back to the surface, without considering the consequences this announcement could trigger. If this kills the deal, okay, let's forget it. It was my mistake. And let me say it again: I apologize.'

To keep me from feeling any worse, he tells me, 'You've just ruined a five-million-pound marketing plan.' They'd planned a surprise reveal, a spectacular presentation on a global scale, with special effects worthy of Hollywood.

I ruined everything with a single Instagram post. But I transferred to Man U anyway. That's the way my relationship with Mino is. We might argue and trade insults, but there's no tearing us apart.

Mino is more than an agent to me, more than a friend – he's a member of my family. That's all. We can go a whole year without speaking, and then when we talk it's as if the last time we saw each other was yesterday. There's not so much as a half-secret between us. We share everything.

For instance, we're both crazy about cars.

I bought a Porsche, a limited edition that you simply can't get your hands on, with the goalie's number one on it – just like old racing cars. A magnificent car. I was lucky to find it. Mino was dreaming of one, too, so I reached out to my contacts and managed to find one for him.

'Here, this is for you. It's a gift. But pay no attention to the number on the doors. The real number one is me.'

Maxwell and I were the first players he worked with, after Pavel Nedvěd.

Mino likes to say, 'Do you know what the difference is between Maxwell and Ibra? If I need money, I call Maxwell and he'll ask me: "How much do you need?" If I call Zlatan, on the other hand, he'll say: "I don't have any – bye." And then he'll hang up. One is a nice guy, and the other one is a bastard.'

But when it's time to negotiate, Mino is the bastard and I'm the nice guy. *Bad cop / good cop*: that's our playbook.

The bastard and the nice guy go to Manchester United. Fantastic first year, because the minute I show up, everyone hates me: Ibra is arrogant, conceited, a hooligan, the guy who never seems to score against English teams, the old man, thirty-five.

Excellent. That's the reaction I'm looking for. Go ahead and hate me. I love it.

While we're still negotiating, I ask the people who are closest to me, 'What do you think about me going to play in the Premier League?'

The first person replies, 'It's a lose-lose situation.'

The second person says, 'It's too fast-paced for you.'

The third person points out, 'If it goes wrong, you'll ruin everything you've achieved in your career.'

The fourth person tells me, 'That's not the right championship.'

Out of seven people I asked, seven advised me against going to England.

I add it all up: they're right, and that's why I'm going to go. Here's the greatest challenge. Buckets of adrenaline.

After three months everyone who hated me has come round to my side. The newspapers are writing positive reviews, interviewing me all the time, asking my opinion and quoting my thoughts.

I liked life in Manchester. I had a beautiful house with a swimming pool, in the area where all the footballers live, just ten minutes away from the training ground. Actually the real swimming pool was the back garden because it rained constantly, and I never really left the house, but that's the way I like it. I mean, even if you do go out in Manchester, where are you going to go? Might as well stay home and play video games.

But one thing surprised me.

Everyone thinks of Man United as a top club, one of the richest and most powerful in the world, and I have to say – viewed from outside – that's how it looked to me, too. But once I got there, I encountered a small, narrow mindset. I could never really figure out whether it was a specific trait of Manchester or was common to all the English.

For instance, take the case of Wayne Rooney, a true sports legend for the club. He stops playing, and the next day they take his name off his locker in the dressing room and empty it, as if he's never existed.

Jesus, that was fast! What's the hurry?

I think to myself: 'If that's the way they treat *him*, after he played more than five hundred matches and scored more than two hundred and fifty goals in the Red Devils shirt, then the day I leave, at the very least, they'll burn my locker to the ground.'

One day I'm at the hotel with the team, before a match. I feel thirsty, I open the minibar and I drink a fruit juice.

We go out to play and then I go home. Time passes. My pay cheque arrives. Normally, I wouldn't even look at the stub. I simply figure out my balance at the end of the year: income versus outlay. That time, though, I don't know why, I felt a little curious and I noticed that they'd subtracted one pound from the total.

I ask the team manager, 'Excuse me, why was that pound deducted?'

She checks and informs me, 'You took a fruit juice from the minibar.'

'You're joking, right?'

'No, anything you consume here, you pay for.'

'Sure, but I wasn't in that hotel minding my own business, I wasn't on holiday – I was on the job. I was there for Man U. If I have to play and I'm thirsty, well, I don't have any choice about drinking – I can't go out on the pitch parched. Plus, I mean, are you kidding? One measly pound?'

Nothing of the sort would ever happen in Italy. At Milan, for any extra expenses I might have run up, Galliani would tell me, 'Don't worry about it. Milan can pay.' And we were rarely talking about a fruit juice from the minibar. If I had an unexpected meeting in Rome, Galliani let me use the company jet and never asked for a penny.

I'm not saying everything ought to be free of charge, but a fruit juice? And you claim to be one of the world's great football clubs? You need to learn from Milan what style is, what constitutes a club's identity. These are the details that make the difference and engender respect among players.

Every day at Man U I'd be asked for my ID before being let into the training ground. I'd roll down my window and tell the guy at the gate, 'Listen, friend, I've been coming here every single day for the past month now. I'm the world's best football player. If you still don't recognize me, you're in the wrong line of work.'

In my second season at Manchester United, in the spring, I wreck my right knee: a tear of the cruciate ligament and the lateral collateral ligament, with detachment of the hamstring.

In April 2017, at a Europa League match against Anderlecht, I jump to head the ball, land badly and my leg crumples unnaturally. I feel a terrible stab of pain and my world falls apart. Darkness. The end.

They operate on me in Pittsburgh in the US, and I explain to my family, 'We can stay together for a week, and then you can go back to Manchester and I'll remain in Sweden.'

'Why?' Helena asks me.

'Because for four months I'm going to have to sweat like an animal, without the slightest distraction. You'd only deprive me of time, energy and focus.'

That's just the way I am. Even when I'm working at the Milanello gym, no one is allowed to distract me. You walk through that door at your own risk. I dive into my own world, and no one can threaten my concentration: I work, I suffer, I work and I suffer.

I have a gym in my house in Stockholm. I call Dario, my personal physio, and ask, 'What do you need?'

'Five large exercise machines.'

I call the company that builds them. 'By tomorrow morning, no later, you need to deliver five of those machines to my home, otherwise I'll be buying them from the competition.'

And the next morning the machines are there, at the agreed hour. Big, hulking giants, weighing almost 500 pounds each.

'Now what?' I ask Dario.

'Seven hours of hard work every day.'

I shut myself up in the gym, without a word to a soul. I let no one into my house and I start pounding away, seven hours a day, staring at my swollen knee. Four months like that, never looking up, and then it's time to go back to Manchester.

I need to see the pitch again, to watch Pogba and my teammates hard at work. For four months I've done individual exercise. Now I need to recover my team spirit, breathe the air of the dressing room again, and get back into my line of sight the object of my efforts, and my suffering: the pitch.

My physio is slightly worried, because he's afraid that we might have gone back to England too soon. We both know that the grey area between gym and playing field is very risky, delicate terrain. If the man guiding me through this process gets something wrong, it can be highly dangerous. During this phase the most important aspect is patience. It's crucial not to be hasty in taking the last step.

I feel fantastic. Mourinho puts me in the hands of a colleague, and he understands how I'm doing. He concentrates into a single week the programme that I was supposed to have stretched out over four weeks. Dario isn't happy. He thinks we're rushing things.

And in fact, even if my knee seems to be working fine, I start to feel pain due to problems with the cartilage, but my adrenaline is pumping so hard that I don't notice it. I'm back on the team after seven months. Seven endless months without a football. I'm as happy as a little boy. I want to play – show the world how good I am.

Mourinho summons me, I play and the English fans go wild over me. I get my new shirt with the number ten, which is Rooney's old number. It's all too great.

But then my adrenaline starts ebbing and I realize something isn't quite right. I talk to my physio about it: I'm in great pain, I don't feel loose or limber, this isn't normal. I have a brand-new knee, fully rebuilt, and I still can't seem to use it properly. I decide to go and talk it over with Mou.

'Coach, don't send me out on the pitch again.'

He's shocked. 'Why not?'

It's not like Ibra to avoid the scrum. He knows me too well for that. I explain, 'Because I'm not the Ibra you used to know. I don't want to lose my teammates' respect. Out of respect for them, I'll come back once I've resolved my problems. I need to work on my own for a little longer. If you send me out there again, I'll only disappoint you.'

Mou replies, 'This is a great act of responsibility on your part, and I say that with full awareness of the size of your ego. I understand that better than others, and I know what this decision costs you, in particular.'

Before you know it, it's January and then February: Man U is facing the decisive phase of the season. Trying to go back out as part of the team in those crucial matches – matches that had to be won at all costs – would have been too stressful. At that point I need different sorts of matches to test out my new knee. I think of the American championship, where so many players go at the end of their careers.

What I need is a less competitive style of football, where I can find my footing without stress, without excessive pressure, to figure out whether I'm still alive and whether I can go back to playing at my old level.

When I was on holiday in Los Angeles I met Jovan Kirovski, a former footballer who had since become the technical director for LA Galaxy. I'd contacted him for help in training Maximilian and Vincent while we were there.

I call him up now and I ask, 'Can I come and work for you guys?'

We talk it over: the MLS has its rules, its budget limits. The Galaxy could only give me a small contract, but that's not a problem – I'm not going there for money. The real problem is that they can't spend much to buy me.

I go and talk to Mourinho and I lay out the whole situation. 'José, you need to get me away from Manchester for free.'

Mou replies like the gentleman he is. 'Considering everything you've done for me, I'm happy to help.'

Mino supports my decision, and so we go to America.

The executives at the Galaxy want to send me out to play right away against Los Angeles FC, a newly founded club. This is going to be the city's first, historic football derby. They work together to speed up all the bureaucratic processes to enable me to get out on the pitch.

I land in California in the evening, with my family and our dog. The next day, on the eve of the derby, I go out for a light training session. I'm half asleep, on account of jetlag.

The fitness coach, who is French, does some kind of test, runs the data through his computer and tells me, 'You're tired.'

'Ah, I'm tired. Seriously?'

The coach agrees. 'Yes, you'd better get some rest, Zlatan. Take your time and get in shape for the upcoming matches.'

'Okay, whatever you say. The coach has the last word.'

The president arrives on the field and I let him know. 'You were in this big hurry and now the coach isn't even going to play me.'

He's astonished. 'He's not going to play you? Hold on, let me talk to him.'

I'm put back on the team sheet the next day and I start on the bench. Soon we're one goal down.

I reassure one of my teammates: 'Don't worry, we're still going to win.'

Then our opponents score again: 2–0.

I repeat, 'Well, it just got harder, but we're still going to win.'

Then they score: 3–0. The teammate beside me on the bench glares at me.

I tell him, 'Better not even take the field today. Let's focus on the next match. This one is done.'

But then, when we're down 3–1, the coach tells me to start warming up. The whole stadium is chanting my name.

It's only twenty minutes to the final whistle.

We immediately score to make it 3–2. Now I can have some fun. I receive the ball forty metres out from the net. I'm in disastrous physical shape. I don't know how my knee is going to react. For sure, I'd never be able to make it to the net at a run. So I let the ball bounce and then kick it on the volley, from midfield.

The ball arcs through the air, right over the head of the goalie, who'd been standing off his line. We're 3–3!

I rip off my shirt and run down the field, both arms wide, while some guy with a television camera on his shoulder comes chasing after me, dragging a mile-long cable behind him: it twists and uncoils like a snake.

The crowd goes wild, and then it goes even wilder when I slot in the winning goal with a header, for a final score of 4–3.

From 0–3 to 4–3, two goals in twenty minutes in my first match, without training and on nine hours of jet-lag, so that my eyelids are practically sagging over my eyeballs.

I'm so tired that at the press conference, all I say is, 'You wanted Zlatan, I gave you Zlatan. You're welcome.' Now let me teach you what football is, because you think that's what you're playing, but real football is something completely different.

The great thing is that, before striking a deal with the Galaxy, I'd been in talks with the other Los Angeles team, the LAFC – that's right, our opponents in the derby – but they decided to sign the Mexican player Carlos Vela instead. Just one more reason to beat them and make it clear, once and for all, who *I* am and who that Mexican is.

In the first four matches I score three goals.

I decide to stay another year in America, and I negotiate my renewal all by myself, without telling Mino, which leaves him fuming, as angry as a wildcat. The worst fight in our career together.

Why did I do it?

Because I was on good personal terms with the owners of the Galaxy, and they were also the owners of the Lakers basketball team and the LA Kings ice-hockey team, as well as plenty of other valuable properties. I was getting along with them just fine, and I didn't want to rock the boat. I was happy with being the highest-paid player in the MLS and having a mansion in Beverly Hills. Here I was, savouring for the first time in so many years the liberty to move freely without being mobbed by my fans. Being a champion in a less popular sport certainly had its advantages. I lived in a house without security gates, I could kick a football around with kids on the beach and they wouldn't recognize me as a star: 'Hey, Mister, you're pretty good at soccer, you know?' I was surrounded by palm trees and sandy beaches, and I felt like I was in heaven.

If Mino had been involved in the negotiations, after my excellent first year in America, he would have demanded everything he could think of – even Lakers stock and a bicycle.

Mino was too powerful for them. He would have slaughtered them, he would have walked out of the room and then I wouldn't have been able to go on playing in the MLS. So I kept him out of it. He really took it hard: 'You shouldn't have done it, Zlatan. That's my job. I should have taken care of it.'

He was right; he was 100 per cent right. But I was afraid of watching the whole deal go sideways. I explained that to him. Mino's never forgiven me. He's still holding on to that grudge today. I disappointed him.

That said, the episode didn't separate us in the slightest. Like all the negative things that have happened throughout all these years, the crisis in Los Angeles only bound us closer together.

At the end of my second year in the States, I decided it was time to call it a day.

Of course Mino disagreed. 'You can't quit now, Zlatan. I still have to go in and steal more money for you, and for me. You need to go back to Europe and prove that you're still Ibra. Even just for one match. You have to show them. Then you can quit.'

And you all know how that went.

Even if I can afford anything I want now, I've always maintained a deep and abiding respect for money. If I see something for ten euros and I think it's only worth seven, I say so: 'Too expensive.'

Every month I personally go over the electricity and gas bills and pay them myself. Every so often I make a wisecrack to Helena: 'The credit card is getting hot. I saw the statement. Slow down a little next month.'

I always travel by private jet. I like to travel feeling relaxed, with no one to bother me. Money can't buy you happiness, but comfort and convenience can. Whereas Helena, if there's no particular urgency, prefers to fly commercial, and tries to save money on her tickets, too.

The first time that our younger son, Vincent, boarded a commercial flight with Helena and saw all the other passengers sitting there, he was astonished. 'Mama, what are all these people doing on our plane?' That's how Helena taught him what privilege means. I have to admit, my wife is very careful about that sort of thing.

Maxi and Vincent have an allowance, so that they can buy snacks at the school cafeteria and pay for any other little expenses they may have. But they're smart kids: if they need something, they ask me or Helena to buy it for them and they never spend their own money.

When I was a kid, I had my own debit card, too. Every month I had a right to seventy-five euros from the Swedish government because I was in school. I didn't know it, because my father never let me have that money. My classmates told me about it: 'Listen, that's your money. You need to ask him for it.'

So I went to my father. 'Hey, how come all my friends get that money, but I don't?'

At first he pretended he didn't know what I was talking about. Then we went to the bank together and he had them issue me a debit card. The government would put those seventy-five euros on the card on the twentieth of every month. At 11.59 p.m. on the nineteenth, I'd be standing in front of the ATM, even if it was snowing and the temperature was below freezing. At the stroke of midnight I'd slide in my card and withdraw my money.

Then I started getting my first pay cheques from the Malmö club – anywhere from 500 to 1,000 euros. I spent my whole first pay cheque on taking an intensive course at the driving school; in just three weeks I would be getting my licence. And then I bought a mobile phone.

The first real blast of adrenaline I got from buying something was the Porsche I purchased in Amsterdam. For a kid who'd grown up in Rosengård, there's nothing more important, nothing more sacred, than a car all your own. I went down to the dealership with my Ajax contract in my hand, to prove that I could afford to finance the vehicle and to have them explain the terms and conditions.

My first year in Turin I went with Helena to sign for the purchase of a Ferrari Enzo. That car was something completely different from anything I'd experienced before – it was mythical. We sat down with the salesman to sign the documents. I'd be making a 10 per cent down-payment. I remember clearly that I was thirsty, and I signed in a hurry so that I could take a drink of water from the glass sitting on the man's desk.

The minute we left the dealership I asked Helena, 'Did you see how much that ten per cent down-payment amounted to?'

'Yes, sixty-five thousand euros.'

It wasn't until then that I realized I'd just bought a €650,000 car.

'Well, I'm glad it's pretty,' I commented.

Cars, as you must have figured out by now, are much more than a passion with me. They are my adrenaline, my escape route to freedom, my personal sensation of power.

I like owning things that other people don't have.

For instance, if you tell me that something exists and it's not available for purchase anywhere, then my brain starts spinning and I need to do anything I can to lay my hands on it. It's a challenge. That goes for cars, too, though they constitute a very special passion, bound up with my past.

In the ghetto, if you wanted to show everyone that you were doing well for yourself, the first thing you wanted to show off was a new car. Because that's when people would say: 'That guy is a success.' There was no more powerful symbol than a flashy car. That's why, still today, I buy lots of cars. The last car I bought was a birthday present for myself when I turned forty.

There was a time when I spent money just like that, without thinking twice. I managed to purchase the house I'd dreamed of when I was a child – the one I'd admired every time I left the ghetto, pedalling along on a stolen bicycle. It was the nicest house in Malmö, the pink villa. That was the most gratifying vindication of my success. I paid a fortune to persuade the people who lived there to move out and make way for me. And when I sold the place, I lost a lot of money.

If you buy with your heart, you're always going to lose money. If you buy with your head, you're probably going to make money.

Now I'm forty, not twenty any more, and when I invest I use my brain. And I never spend money unless I'm convinced it's a good deal for me. Take the house I made by remodelling an old church. I paid a bargain price for it.

Helena is an expert in fashion and design, and she furnished it beautifully. She's good at it, she has fine taste and she knows what she's doing. I don't understand much about it, but whenever she asks my opinion about some specific detail of furnishing or interior design, I pretend to think it over and maybe I'll grunt and say, 'Huh, I don't really know . . .' Like that, making sure I don't give her too much satisfaction.

This building in the heart of Stockholm had really caught our eye. It was a church from the late nineteenth century. We bought it and renovated it over the course of the years, counting on the possibility that we might want to live there for good when my football career ended.

It's a five-storey house, with anything you care to think of inside. If a war breaks out, we'll be able to survive just fine. As long as someone brings us food, that is.

I overdid it, Ibra-style. I bought the whole structure so that I could turn it into a single residence. And I mean, after all, where does a god live? In a church.

This, too, is a wonderful moral victory. Someone who comes from poverty, like me, has pitched his tent in a neighbourhood filled with fat cats.

*

When it comes to naming boats, people use flashy, pompous names from films: *Black Legend*, *Gold Star*, *Lady Mary* . . . I thought to myself: 'I'm going to call my boat *Unknown*. That way, anyone who sees it will wonder: "What kind of idiot names his boat *Unknown*? What the hell kind of a name is that?" Then I step out onto the deck and they exclaim: "Well, fuck, that's Ibrahimović!"'

The boat is unknown, okay, but the owner is very much known. I loved the idea of creating that contrast. The boat is *Unknown*, but me, I'm *well known*. If you ask me, it's a perfect name.

I bought the boat so that I could enjoy the sea in perfect freedom, travelling from one port to another with my family. In a time of Covid, it's also an extra security factor. I didn't know whether my sons would appreciate it. But in fact the minute we got out on the boat for the first time, they were thrilled: four or five uninterrupted hours in the water.

After a while, though, we realized that the boat was a little too small for our needs and we upgraded to a bigger boat, one that suited us better. That's what we want the boat for: to live on the sea, not to show off in ports.

The new boat is named *Unknown*, too. Of course it isn't an investment, it's a direct cost. Money isn't only good for making more money – it's also a way of enjoying life.

I had an apartment in New York in the Trump SoHo complex in Manhattan, a luxury hotel with apartments, spas and top-flight services. The very best. When I wasn't going to be there, I'd rent it out. It was a great bargain, a real opportunity. Then Donald Trump became president of the United States and the Trump SoHo emptied out. No one wanted to stay there any more. There were strikes and protest marches. I was forced to sell my apartment, because no one wanted to rent there. I lost half my investment. Sooner or later Trump is going to have to reimburse me for my loss.

I have consultants who work at finding investment opportunities in every corner of the world. When they alert me to one, we have a meeting, we examine it and then we come to a decision together. This creates adrenaline, too. I don't just put in the money. I like being hands-on with the project, watching it grow from a seed.

Together with Maxwell, Verratti and Sirigu, I've founded a company, with me as the majority shareholder, which has invested in a private equity fund. Here, too, I like to be directly involved in the business and talk to my financial consultants, talk to the brokers. I make an effort to know, learn and enquire. I always want to maintain complete control over the situation. I'm not handing anyone a bag full of my money and telling them, 'Use it as you think best.' No, I'm taking part in the decisions and I'm judging the risks.

The Padel Zenter in Stockholm, for instance, is going great guns and I'm planning to open another one soon in Milan, with nineteen courts. And then there's the forest land I bought, for hunting and nature expeditions. I used to go on hunting trips and paid for the privilege, but the cost was so extreme that my friends couldn't afford it any longer. So I bought some forest land where they can hunt for free. On the island in Lake Malar, for the most part, what we have are stags, mouflons and wild boar. In the forest up north, near Norway, there are hares, elks and bears.

Hunting represents the adrenaline of adventure; it's feeling free in nature, it's a primitive challenge against an animal: you with your intelligence, the animal with its instincts. You have to seek it, study its movements, its track and spoor, sniff the wind, catch scents. It's not as easy as you might think, especially in my forest land, which is not fenced in and extends for miles and miles – an enormous property. The animal can escape and run to safety.

All things considered, I feel like them. I live on instinct, I need freedom.

I need escape.

6. The Journalist
(or About Communication)

There was an episode that made me change my attitude towards the press – specifically, an article. In fact it wasn't even really an article; it was only a small item, a green box in the sports pages of *Aftonbladet*, a popular Swedish newspaper. I was twenty-one years old and I was playing for Ajax.

Until that day I'd revealed myself to sports journalists as I was, without filters and without any particular worries. I'd always been myself, the way I normally like to be. At first I enjoyed reading what they had to say about me. This was a new game. And I was proud of it, naturally.

I remember what a thrill it was the first few times I saw my name and my picture in the newspapers. I'd cut out the photos and keep them; and then I stopped and my father took over the job for me. He'd frame every cutting and hang them on the living-room walls, and he kept doing it until one day I had to tell him, 'Papa, put them all in another room, not in the living room. It looks like you live in a museum.'

Nowadays I like it when I see my children stopping in front of those pictures and press cuttings. They look at them, read them, comment upon them between themselves. It really does seem as if they're touring a museum – the museum of their father.

Anyway, let's get back to the start of my career, when everything was just beginning. I had set out to conquer the world, and even the newspapers that wrote about me were part of the festivities, part of this new adventure, and they contributed to the thrill, and to my growing sense of excitement. Every evening I'd wait for the sports section of the news broadcast to see if they mentioned my name. When they did, I'd go to sleep with a smile on my face. Then came that brief little item in *Aftonbladet*.

I was on a sports retreat with the Swedish national team. I chatted about this and that with a journalist, including the fact that, every now and then, I sometimes felt a little lonely in Amsterdam. That's normal – I was far from home. 'If I had a girlfriend, the situation would be quite different,' I put out there casually. No one knew about Helena yet, as we'd taken great care to keep our romance under cover for some time.

The next day, adjacent to the interview, the newspaper published a sort of personal classified ad under the headline 'Do you want to win the Champions League with me?' They wrote something that ran more or less like this: *Athletic young man, age 21, 6 foot 6 inches tall, 185 pounds, looking for a woman the right age to begin a serious relationship. I don't smoke or drink and I love nice cars. I like kids. I live in Amsterdam: where do you live? Write care of the Swedish Football Association.*

They even published the actual address of the Swedish Football Association. There were plenty of readers who didn't understand that it was a hoax and wrote in to it.

Okay, it was nothing but a prank, but I really took offence at that nonsense. As soon as the guy who'd done the interview tried to apologize, I yelled at him, calling him a clown, said that he'd disrespected me and hurled a lot of other choice insults. For years I refused to talk to anyone who wrote for that publication.

I'd only answer their questions at Swedish national team press conferences, but I stopped giving them exclusive interviews. I'd tell them only the basics; I was serious and controlled, and I no longer laughed or kidded around, the way I used to; I no longer answered their questions with the first thing that came to mind, on instinct. I stopped revealing myself. I'd donned a suit of armour to protect myself.

After that, sport journalists in Sweden started writing that I was behaving like a diva, that I didn't know how to play along and be part of the group; that I had an exaggerated self-image, I was all talk and I'd never amount to a thing. I remember all the journalists who wrote things like that, one by one. I know their names. They were forced to eat their words, because I was a success everywhere I went; and everywhere I went I was the leader of the group. They wrote, and they continue to write, about the role I played on the Swedish national team: that I'm an egotist, an individualist and that I have no respect for the system. But I've won more titles collectively than all the other players on the Swedish national team put together. That means that if there's anyone who knows how to win with a team, it would be me.

I soon learned that the little game that the press likes to play is to build you up and then tear you down. At first I asked my more experienced teammates on the Swedish national team for advice – teammates like, say, Henrik Larsson. How should I behave with the media?

All of them told me, 'Zlatan, we've never had the kind of attention from the press that you have, and we've never been in the situation you're going through. None of us can give you any advice.'

And so from that moment on I decided to act on instinct, taking only my own counsel, when it came to the press. To learn from my own experience and my own mistakes.

I remember that at the end of a Swedish national team match, back when I was playing for Ajax, someone interviewed me live. The journalist started asking me questions about a certain tactical problem that we'd encountered on the pitch, and I gave him my answer. He wasn't satisfied. He changed the words he used, but continued hammering at me on the same topic, four or five times in a row.

So I got fed up and, in a live broadcast, offered my solution: 'Listen, you go out on the pitch and try it yourself. Okay?'

In the Netherlands, at first they didn't know exactly who I was, or how good I was. I remember one journalist asking me, 'When you're playing away games, do they jeer and whistle at you?'

'Everyone does,' I replied.

'Then that must mean you're good,' he reasoned.

I played well against Milan in the Amsterdam summer tournament and I immediately started to hear comparisons with van Basten. The pressure built. If I made any sort of mistake in a match, the crowd would jeer and whistle and the newspapers would criticize me viciously. They expected me to play at van Basten's level all the time. But I was only twenty.

My image changed in Sweden once I won the Jerring Award in 2008. It's a prestigious prize given to the best Swedish athlete. It's decided by a vote of ordinary people, choosing from ten candidates.

A footballer had never won it before, though it had been won by the Swedish national team for its third-place finish at the American World Cup in 1994. But never by a single player. I wept when I was awarded that prize.

Since that day Swedes started looking at me with different eyes. Real people, I mean. Not journalists. To them, I was always a bad boy, a prima donna, a rotten apple. But, as I always say, you're never going to win the war against the press.

In 2014 the newspaper *Dagens Nyheter* drew up a list of the greatest Swedish athletes of all time. I came in second, just behind Björn Borg. I was asked for a comment. I answered, 'As far as I'm concerned, coming in second is like coming in last. With all my respect for the other athletes, I'd have called first place for Ibrahimović, and then in second place Ibrahimović, third place Ibrahimović, fourth place Ibrahimović and fifth place Ibrahimović.'

That comment was read back to Borg, who started

laughing. 'Ibra is a funny guy, a lovely individual. And anyway he's better known around the world than Ikea, and a lot more famous than I was back in the day.'

Naturally I was kidding. Borg is the only Swedish sports figure I was truly happy to meet: 'Fuck, that's Borg.' I mean, a guy who won five times at Wimbledon and six times at Roland-Garros in Paris. Really I'd made a wisecrack. But I wasn't entirely joking. The truth is that, for Swedish journalists, putting the very non-Swedish surname Ibrahimović ahead of everyone else was a source of considerable pain.

The same thing happened when I beat Sven Rydell's all-time record of forty-nine goals and became the top scorer in the history of the Swedish national team. That record had stood for eighty years. Now the top of the heap featured the surname Ibrahimović – and no longer a Swedish name. Today it might have gone differently, as the younger generations are more accustomed to the idea of a multi-ethnic society. But at the time it didn't go down well at all.

In Amsterdam I made friends with a journalist, Thijs Slegers. He interviewed me for *Voetbal International* and he struck me as a pretty nice guy. We used to play tennis together and we'd also occasionally go out and about. In my early days in the Netherlands I knew practically no one. Thijs helped me out and, above all, put me in touch with Mino Raiola.

I don't like having personal relationships with the press. If they want interviews, then they have to reach out to the club or my sponsors. I never give a journalist my phone number. If one of them manages to get it and texts me, I don't bother to answer. No one dares ask me for information or offer suggestions about the team formation. If one of my teammates leaks things from inside the dressing room to the press, in the hope of getting better coverage, it's best that I never find out about it. Best for him, that is.

The dressing room is my home. And in my home I need to be able to feel free to speak and act as I please, without fear that outsiders might be informed.

The same principle applies to what happens out on the pitch. I don't read the sports papers, except perhaps for a quick glance at the headlines. Every now and then someone will mention an article about me, for better or worse. If I happen to decide that I need to take a stance about something, I let Mino know and he deals with it.

The report cards that the press issues about matches are of no interest to me. I've seen bad grades given when I played well, and excellent grades when I played poorly. I can judge myself without help from anyone else – I don't need to know what other people think. Only insecure players worry about Monday-morning report cards.

As I've said before: in my opinion, ex-players who become journalists or television commentators only do it because they are thirsty for attention and are afraid of being forgotten. Not for the adrenaline. If you're coming in from the pitch, you're never going to find adrenaline sitting on a stool and wearing a headset.

I once tried working as a TV commentator, for beIN

SPORTS, during the Russian World Cup. I was definitely not comfortable with it. I felt as if I was the ex-player being asked to critique the players who were still actually playing. I had a contract with Qatar TV, but after the first match I told them, 'Listen, sorry, I'm not cut out for this. I can't do it. You can keep the money you owe me. I don't want to be paid.'

As I mentioned, I have a team of consultants to look after my business interests and a pool of specialists to keep an eye on every aspect of my professional football endeavours, but I don't have an expert per se to look after PR and communications. I don't need anyone dispensing magical potions to enhance my personal image or make my life appear to be brimming over with happiness. Not like so many of my fellow players. I rely on my own personal rule, which applies in most cases: 'It's enough to be myself, and I'm perfect the way I am.'

Anything I post on a digital platform I put together myself. I've read extensively, I've asked around, I've learned things to my satisfaction. All the pictures and words that I publish on Instagram are my own creation. Every now and then someone gets in touch to ask for payment for the rights to the pictures that I use. It strikes me as strange: people use my image on all the platforms on Earth without paying me a cent, and then I'm supposed to pay for the pictures I post?

I've had my fun with the English media, as mentioned previously. They met me with their rifles levelled: the bad boy, the arrogant player, the footballer who'd never score against an English team.

After three months at Manchester United they put flowers in the barrels of their rifles. They kept calling me for interviews, or even for a brief opinion on any and every topic imaginable. I was happy to talk to everyone, but at a certain point I had to say: 'Enough is enough. Sorry, guys, but I need to focus on my job.'

My relationship with French journalists has been more complicated, on account of my ill-advised comments in Bordeaux and the fact that the wealthy PSG team was not well liked and was the target of great jealousy. I made an effort to explain certain things, but the media invariably put it in personal terms. They either failed to understand or pretended not to. In the end I stopped trying. It was pointless to waste so much energy on futile attempts at communication.

On the other hand, press conferences are my idea of fun.

I feel like I'm in an arena: me against everyone. I never place limits on the questions. The journalists can ask me whatever they like, but they'd better be ready for my answers. And they need to know that the quality of the answer is conditional on the quality of the question: if the question is stupid, my answer will be just as stupid.

Once, during a press conference, a Swedish journalist stood up and left because he wasn't satisfied with my answers. Anyone who does that is a weakling. And misguided.

Swedish journalists are generally quite timid at press conferences, because they're afraid of my answers and what I might think of their questions. So they don't ask many. I've even found myself being forced to prompt them:

'There's so many of you, and you only ask a couple of questions? Are you sure? Come on now. Don't you want to ask any other questions? Okay, have a nice day.' Then I stand up and leave.

Italian journalists, in contrast, are more aggressive. They ask you questions about anything and everything. They're fearless.

As soon as I went back to Milan one female journalist asked, 'Everyone who's come back to Milan for a second tour has turned out badly. Why won't you turn out to be a failure, too?'

'Because I'm not like everybody else,' I answered her.

Things went far worse with another female television journalist about ten years previously. It was March 2012, at the San Siro. After the match with Lecce, which we won 2–0, I stopped for a series of TV interviews on the pitch. She asked me something that got under my skin, about an argument that I was supposed to have had with Allegri. I replied brusquely, cutting off her questions and moving on to a different broadcaster. But the journalist didn't leave. She probably got mad, and she waited for me to finish the other interview to ask me further questions.

She kept staring, her eyes glued on me. I noticed her while I was answering the questions of the other journalist and it annoyed me. At a certain point, during a live feed, I turned to her and asked, 'The fuck you looking at?' Of course those words went out over the airwaves.

Once I was done with the interview, she gestured at me as if to say: 'Shut up, shut your mouth' or something of the sort.

I shot my elastic hairband at her, because she'd really pissed me off. Milan then sent her a bouquet of roses in my name as an apology, and that got me even madder, because I feel it's up to me whether or not I want to apologize. Like the time I had a fight with Lukaku and someone from Milan suggested, 'They'll get together over an espresso.'

What? An espresso? With Lukaku? You'd better not even try to get me in the same room with him.

But that's another story.

The Zlatan of today would have apologized to the journalist; actually, he never would have insulted her in the first place. Back then I was so much younger and really immature. If I think back to that scene and the things I said to her, I feel like an idiot. I'm sorry about it.

I have absolutely no problem with female journalists writing about football. In fact I think it's right and proper and admirable that they do so.

One thing I really enjoyed was American talk shows, because they were truly fun interviews and they'd let me do whatever I liked. They seemed to be terrified of making me feel awkward and they did all they could to put me at my ease. 'We can send you the questions that we'll ask during the broadcast a few days ahead,' they'd volunteer.

I'd respond, 'There's no need, thanks. I don't want to know the questions in advance. That doesn't seem fair.'

'But all our guests ask for them – actors, singers, politicians. They don't want to be caught off-guard. They don't want to look foolish.'

So I'd explain, 'Don't worry. I'll answer spontaneously, with whatever pops into my head, then and there. I'll be myself, so I can't possibly look foolish.'

Once, before I went on, in a TV studio in Los Angeles, the head of production kept hammering at me with unasked-for advice: 'Do this, do that. You know, lots of athletes freeze up when they sit down on that couch in front of the TV camera.'

I told him, 'Listen, just open the door and you'll see: when I walk on, that TV show will become *my* TV show. Everyone else will disappear. Enjoy it . . .'

And so it was, on *Jimmy Kimmel Live!* and on all the other popular talk shows that I went on. I told Jimmy Kimmel about viewing a mansion in Beverly Hills right after we first got to America. Helena liked it and wanted to sign the contract and move in straight away. 'There's only one problem. It's not furnished,' she said.

'We can buy furniture at Ikea,' I suggested.

Our real-estate agent weighed in with a smirk of faint indignation. 'Rich people here don't go to Ikea.'

'Smart people do,' I retorted.

On *The Late Late Show with James Corden* they subjected me to the 'Can Zlatan . . . ?' test, to prove that I was capable of doing anything. They asked me to twist the top off a jar of pickles; they asked me to list the names of all Kim Kardashian's husbands; they had me say 'Zlatan Ibrahimović' with my mouth full of marshmallows; and then they had me do the Floss. I really enjoyed myself with James, and the little sketches we did together were great fun.

TV shows invited me on because I worked well on

television and the audience response was always great. I know that when I'm allowed to be myself, I'm quite a spectacle – whether on the pitch or on a talk show.

I started out on a godforsaken field in the south of Spain when I was just nineteen, shouting, 'Showtime! Showtime!' and I haven't stopped since.

7. The Goal
(*or About Happiness*)

When I score a goal, I throw both arms up in the air and I feel alive, I feel like the king of the world. I can't hug every single spectator in the stands, one by one, so I throw my arms wide and it's as if I'm hugging them all at once. Then my teammates surround me to celebrate. They're all shorter than me. I lower my arms and gather them under my wings, like an angel.

But I don't always celebrate like that. Sometimes I run, at other times I leap straight up and punch the air, and sometimes I tear off my shirt while running at top speed. It depends on how much adrenaline is pumping in my bloodstream; it depends on what my instincts tell me to do.

People always ask what I feel after scoring a goal. It's impossible to answer that question, because no two goals are alike. Every single goal gives me a unique, exclusive thrill. Each goal makes me lose control. In half a second a hundred different things to do unfold in my head, then the ball drops into one of the slots on the roulette wheel and I do that exact thing, without even having chosen it.

Likewise, my instincts choose a single spectator.

I don't have a shapeless wall of people in front of me. When I celebrate a goal, I focus on just one face, and it may belong to a man, a girl, a little boy or an old man.

I savour their happiness, I put that happiness in contact with my own and I let them communicate. It's as if I'd played and scored for that person – and that person alone. We remain connected for a brief instant and then, as soon as the adrenaline drops, that face vanishes, melting into all the others. I forget it, and the spectators turn back into a bright, colourful wall.

When Maxi and Vincent score goals, I'm proud like any father who is happy that his children are successful. And, to an even greater extent, I'm delighted with their joy. But the younger one has surprised me.

As I've said, when Vincent scores a goal he's happy. But when he can assist one of his teammates to score a goal, he's happier still.

At his age, you'd usually expect a youngster to be filled with the pride and desire to show off his own qualities, to let the world see how good he is. The satisfaction of sharing in the joy of others is a very grown-up idea. Children tend to be more selfish. One day I talked to him about it and I asked him, playfully, 'Vincent, are you sure you're my son?'

Maxi is more like me, and when a teammate scores a goal he says, 'Well, sure, even a child could have scored that one.' And then, if it's Maxi scoring the goal, he throws both arms wide, the same way I do.

When I see the two of them playing football I'm happy, because I imagine they're experiencing the joy I felt when I was their age, even if their world is so different from how mine was. My father was suffering over the war in the former Yugoslavia; my mother worked hard from dawn to nightfall; I never had enough to eat, and I always wore the same tracksuit. As for school, forget about it . . . If I played football any chance I got, it was partly to shut my eyes to all of that. Football was my only form of happiness – the only part of my life where I felt free of problems.

I scored my first goals, in the garden of Rosengård, in a goal made of three industrial metal pipes, without a net. Everything there had to be indestructible in order to withstand, as well as possible, the vandals who haunted that ghetto. The fencing around the pitch was iron, a large, heavy hurricane fence. You went in and you felt like you were in prison, or in an enclosure for animals that would never be able to escape.

Back then, like everyone in Sweden, I went crazy with joy over Kennet Andersson's goal at the US World Cup in 1994. Kennet, who would later play in Italy as well, leapt higher than the gloves of the Romanian goalie and scored with a header to make it 2–2 in extra time. I was thirteen years old.

The thrill of scoring a goal in the shirt of the Swedish national team is very special – it's like planting a flag on the globe, it's like shouting, 'We are Swedes.'

If I score while wearing the yellow shirt, I know that I'm making everyone happy, from the fishermen of Gotland to the children of Kiruna, and not only the spectators in one stadium or the fans of one club. It's a powerful sensation that pumps so much adrenaline into my veins. So you can just imagine when, wearing that shirt in 2012, I let fly with four solid punches at England.

Thanks to Kennet Andersson's goal, we made it to penalties in 1994, eliminating Romania and making it to the World Cup semi-final against the great Brazilian national team, with the young Ronaldo at the centre of it.

When I was a boy, there was no player who thrilled me like 'The Phenomenon'. I would watch his goals and feints over and over again on the internet. Then I'd run out to replay them myself on the sand of the Rose Garden, aiming at the iron poles in the animal enclosure.

If I'm going to make a list of all the goals of my career, I'll start with the goal at La Manga. It is still one of my finest, scored at the very beginning of the whole story, when everything was just getting started.

March 2001: a friendly in preparation for the Swedish championship on this strip of land in the middle of the sea, in southern Spain near Murcia. The sun is shining – nothing like the Swedish chill. It's nice out there. We're playing against the Norwegians of Moss. I'm nineteen.

It's a special exhibition game because I know that people have come to see me from Ajax, a team that's been taking a look at me – and not merely any two people from the team, but the coach of the first team, Jacobus 'Co' Adriaanse, in person, and the famous Leo Beenhakker, who has coached Real Madrid and has now come back to the Dutch team as sports director.

We go on the attack. I'm off to the left. I call for the ball and I receive a fast pass. I don't stop the ball. Instead I put down my foot so that the ball slams against it, pops straight up and flies over the heads of my opponents.

I sprint forward, run past them, catch up with the ball and hit it with my heel straight up over the head of another Norwegian. Before it can hit the ground, I kick it in mid-air with my left foot and send it like an arrow into the net.

Adriaanse, who is right behind the goal, gives me a strange look. He seems frightened by what he's witnessed. Beenhakker is sitting in the stands with his usual grim expression.

I run the length of the pitch shouting, because I'm more surprised than anybody by the incredible thing I've just managed to pull off: two sombreros . . . It all happened instinctively. I wouldn't even have been able to dream up a goal of that sort.

A journalist who was there at La Manga wrote the next day that, while I was rejoicing, I kept shouting my own name: 'Zlatan! Zlatan!' He got it wrong. He couldn't have been further from the truth. While I was running the length of the field I was shouting: 'Showtime! Showtime!' Because that goal really had been quite a show – spectacular. And it wasn't long before Ajax signed me.

I also remember the beautiful first goal in the Champions League that I scored while wearing the white-and-red shirt of AFC Ajax, the Lancers. We were playing in Amsterdam against Lyon, in September 2002. It was my first night in the Champions League. I had achieved a dream.

At a certain point I face off against the Brazilian José Edmílson, a defender who only a few months before this has become a world champion. We're both in the penalty area, off to the left of the goal. I pretend to go towards the goal line to cross the ball, but instead I dart towards the centre and shoot diagonally: goalpost, net.

I once saw Zidane pull off a move like that. I tried it, the same way that back in the Rose Garden I tried to repeat the exploits of Ronaldo 'The Phenomenon'. It worked for me exactly as it had for Zidane. I ran eighty metres, because I'd obtained pitchside seats for friends of mine who were in town from Malmö, but at the far side of the field, and I wanted to celebrate with them. A goal in the Champions League is special because there are so few matches. Whatever you're going to do, you'll have to do it there, that night. You can't say the way you can in the league: 'Oh well, I'll score next week.'

Your opponents are special, too, as you're not going to play against them all the time. You're playing against the best teams there are. Even the ball is different – spangled with stars. A Champions League match is like a Sunday in the middle of the week, and scoring a goal in one has a special flavour, sweeter than the rest.

But even a friendly in August can thrill you and pump up your adrenaline, especially if you're playing in a top-flight stadium against a first-class opponent: Benfica–Juve, at Lisbon's Estádio da Luz, 'the Cathedral'. Summer 2005, the start of my second season in Turin.

A ball comes my way from the left. I'm more than a hundred metres from the goal, I control it with my chest and then I make up my mind: I'm going to shoot from here. I let fly with a perfect left-footed volley, a bomb, and it sails right into the top corner. The goalie can't do a thing. Sitting in the Benfica dugout is Ronald

Koeman, my old coach at Ajax. He knows that I can score that kind of goal.

Among the goals I scored with Inter, naturally I'd choose the double in the rain at Parma, on the last day of the 2007–8 championship. I start the match on the bench because one of my knees is hurting. We have to win, but we don't seem able to score. It feels as if we're under some kind of a curse. Then Mancini sends me on in the second half: *boom, boom,* two goals, and we walk off with the Scudetto in our pocket.

In my list of lifetime best goals I'd also include the two against Arsenal while wearing the Barcelona shirt, in the 2009–10 Champions League, which was won by Inter, a team I'd just left. It was a match that was insanely intense. Guardiola had given me an order: 'The minute their goalie gets the ball, you go straight for him – attack!' We were pressing anything that moved on the pitch.

I see two different balls coming at me, practically identical, both dropping vertically, and I let each one drop by my side. I guide the first ball gently over the goalie's head, and I fire the second one just under the crossbar. And this against the English, who always say that I can't score against them. Twice as sweet.

From the year of the Scudetto at Milan, I'd choose the goal against Genoa, in a home match. Pirlo makes a perfect long pass, I run between Dario Dainelli and Andrea Ranocchia as they start to squeeze me, then I extend my leg until I'm doing the splits and I beat the goalie with a lob. Seconds later, Gattuso is all over me, grabbing my head in both hands and screaming into my face like a lunatic. He must have smacked me while he was at it. I really loved it when he riled me up like that. Rino was a human adrenaline-bomb drifting around the pitch.

In that championship, in Lecce, I scored a goal that was identical to the one I scored against Benfica with Juve, from thirty metres. There were some who said that I simply kicked it randomly. Nonsense! I'd seen perfectly well where the goalie was: too far off his line.

The one who went crazy that time was Adriano Galliani. That man was always terribly stressed out during our matches. I worried about his health and I'd tell him, over and over again, 'Boss, as long as you have Ibra, you can stay there, seated and relaxed.'

He'd reply, all anxious and worked up, 'All right, Ibra. All right, Ibra.'

We'd win, he'd rejoice, he'd come down to the dressing room and go crazy with joy. I have a good relationship with Galliani. We're adrenaline brothers.

As my Parisian pearl, I'll take the double at the first match against Marseille, in 2012. I'd only just arrived in Ligue 1. Playing for Olympique de Marseille was the African defender who later went to Torino FC, Nicolas N'Koulou. For days the media had been saying, 'N'Koulou is the only player in France who can stop Ibrahimović.'

All right. We'll see.

Corner kick at the start of the match. I run to meet the ball, I beat N'Koulou to it, I deliver a Taekwondo tackle right under his nose and I shoot into the net. Then I also score a thirty-metre free kick.

After each goal, I get the ball out of the net and carry it fast back to the centre circle, exactly as my physio asked me to do: 'Zlatan, would you do something for me? Whenever you score a goal that gives you the lead, get hold of the ball immediately and take it back to the centre circle. It's like saying: "That goal wasn't enough for me. You're such a weak team that I'm hungry to score even more against you." Do that and you'll see, it'll make them boil with rage.'

Gift delivered.

And I gave Manchester United the gift of two cups as soon as I got there. It was the start of August 2016, my first official match with the Red Devils, the FA Community Shield (between the winners of the Premiership and the FA Cup in the previous season) against the surprisingly competitive Leicester under Claudio Ranieri. We take the lead through Jesse Lingard, then Jamie Vardy evens the score in the second half. There's a whiff of extra time in the air. But at minute eighty-three I climb up Wes Morgan's broad back and, with a header, I nod in the winning goal.

The red part of Wembley went crazy. They had just found out who Ibra is. It wasn't a bad start.

A few months later, in February 2017, I offer an encore in the final match of the League Cup against Southampton. I score a penalty, Lingard makes it 2–0 and the story seems to come to an end right there. But no: the Italian player Manolo Gabbiadini equalizes with a lovely double. There's another whiff of extra time in the air. Once again, a few minutes short of the ninetieth minute, I bring victory in the final with a headed goal. Once again, the enormous red patch of Manchester fans explodes in a roar.

That's a deep and electrifying thrill, partly because anything that happened at Manchester United was bound to echo around the world. It was a distinct, special sensation, unlike anything I've ever experienced anywhere else. If someone sneezed at Man U, five minutes later everyone knew about it in China and every other corner of the planet. That's what made it such a powerful club.

I hadn't just sneezed; I'd won two cups for my new team, with three decisive goals in the sacred temple of Wembley.

I'd also add to that list the goal I scored against Lazio on my return to the pitch after four months out for an injury. It was September 2021. 'The easiest goal of your life,' everyone says now. Okay, but who created that goal? Not Rebić, but me, with my movement. If I'd merely stood still, Ante wouldn't have been able to do a thing with that ball. The goal wasn't simply a quick tap in on the goal line; it was a good idea hatched long before, in my head.

Anyway, even if it's an easy one, any goal you score after a lengthy period of recovery is still huge. It means one more step towards being fully healed, getting back into the game; and it means putting all your memories of the injury a little further behind you – in that instance, at the age of thirty-nine. Seeing that ball sail into the Lazio net did me a world of good.

A goal is always essential for an attacker, even if, truth be told, that wasn't necessarily the case for me at the beginning of my career. I was mainly focused on playing well and, when it came to choosing my moves, I was selfish, looking for the most spectacular that would put me in the spotlight. Showtime! Then van Basten and Capello helped me understand the fundamental importance of a goal.

But I've never been an obsessive fanatic of scoring – one of those guys who'll shoot from any angle – because my chief interest has always been playing football. If I manage to get in position in front of the goal, I'm not only thinking of putting the ball in the net. No. If I see a teammate who is better positioned than I am, I'll pass him the ball: that's what it means to play football.

I always ask any young footballer I meet two basic questions. The first one is: 'What position are you going to play? Defender, midfielder, right-winger . . . Okay.' The second question: 'If you manage to arrive in front of goal with a teammate who's in a better position than you are, are you going to try to score or are you going to pass to him?'

The right answer is the second option.

Everyone thinks of me as a selfish person, someone who thinks only of himself and considers himself to be all-powerful. In a way, it's true, but when I'm out on the pitch I play football. If I need to pass the ball to a teammate, I don't hesitate to do so, and it's partly to prove that I'm above the mere obsession with goals – that I'm bigger than the person who actually scores the goal.

It's one thing to celebrate a goal, it's another thing to be in desperate need of one. If you're in desperate need, you're not really going to enjoy the game. I've played with teammates who were on edge because they hadn't scored, even if we'd won 5–0. No, I'm not talking about Pippo Inzaghi. Let me say a word in his defence. For Pippo, scoring was everything, because it was the only thing he knew how to do. It made sense that Pippo would go after goals so stubbornly. If he didn't score, then he wouldn't be Inzaghi. And then what would he be?

Today a goal no longer constitutes my greatest source of satisfaction, and I proved that by letting Franck Kessié take the penalty against Roma. I made that decision. I'm gratified when I can give something to other people, I help my team through the game, I feel that I'm a leader in a different, more mature way. Then, if I have a chance to score 100 goals, obviously, I'll score 200 of them.

I scored a goal against Lazio with my boots untied. Not one boot, but both of them. I don't know how those laces could have come undone at the same instant. Nothing like it's ever happened before. Go figure.

I see the ball coming straight towards our goal and I say to myself: 'This would be a good time to tie my laces.' I kneel down, but then we immediately regain possession of the ball, Sandro Tonali passes to Rebić and there we are: two against two. So I stand up and run towards the goal with both boots untied. There, one of my teammates is all alone, against two Lazio players. I react instinctively to try to break one of his opponents away, so that he's only dealing with one man. Then we can see what happens next, right? I make my move, he passes the ball to me and I score a goal.

The instinct that led me to stand up with my laces undone wasn't hunger for a goal, it was an impulse to give a helping hand to a teammate in trouble. I didn't say to myself: 'Ooh, goody, here's a goal for me.' No, I thought: 'He's got two opponents coming at him – let me go and help him out.' I thought about my teammate, and the goal arrived by dumb luck. If I'd thought only about the goal, maybe it would never have happened.

I scored with a samurai plait on my head. I wanted to come up with something symbolic for my return to the pitch after such a long time. I'm like Samson: the longer my hair, the stronger I feel. And that's something I use to my own advantage.

I mentioned this earlier: when I was little, my father and I would always watch Bruce Lee and Jackie Chan movies, so I developed a passion for Asian martial-arts films. That's where the samurai plait comes from. Lots of people since then have posted my picture next to one of Tao Pai Pai from *Dragon Ball*, the Japanese manga. Truth be told, we do resemble each other.

But it isn't easy to do a proper plait. The secret is to pull the hair back really tight before plaiting, make sure it's smooth and flat, and then tie it good and tight; otherwise, when you're running the plait will come loose.

I thought: 'What I need here is an expert on this kind of hairstyle.' People recommended a hairdresser of Senegalese descent who specialized in multi-ethnic hairstyles. She came to see me for a try-out, and I immediately understood that she was the right person. She wasn't afraid. When attaching my extensions, she pulled on them as if she wanted to rip them out of my head. There you go – that's how you do it.

I asked her, 'Could you come to the hotel on the day of the match?'

She immediately accepted. 'Okay, give me the address.'

At the San Siro you'll see Ibra again: the goalmouth samurai.

A goal is the joy of the game, and children are the joy of your life. But a few months before Maximilian was born, I was overcome by panic. Worse panic every day.

In the end I talked to Helena about it. 'Listen, I don't know if I'm ready.'

'Neither do I, but let's not think about it too much,' she answered.

So we get to the clinic. I can't really handle hospitals, in the first place. I get a knot in my throat and I feel like I'm about to suffocate. I can't breathe. What's more, this was my first son about to be born. Helena is calm, and I'm simply a wreck from all the stress.

Then the epidural failed to work and she went into a panic. I took her hand, I talked to her, I did everything I could think of to reassure her. 'It'll be fine, wait and see. Keep calm, I'm here with you . . .'

But she kept crying and, at a certain point, I was afraid I was going to explode from the tension. I could feel a volcano building up inside me. I felt like shouting, 'Stop snivelling! Let's go into that room, have our baby and get the hell out of this damned hospital. I can't breathe in here!' Instead of comforting her, I was about to freak out.

Then Maxi came into the world. And I burst out crying.

He was so tiny and strange, all purple in the face. They cleaned him up and gave him to me. He was screaming and I didn't know how to get him to stop. I called the nurses, the obstetricians – everybody within sight. I was afraid that he wasn't well, and I didn't know what to do. I was afraid that something might be happening, partly because, when I was born, the nurse who was holding me dropped me on the floor, from about three feet in the air. But as the minutes passed, the baby took on a more normal coloration and I started to calm down, too. I smiled at him and he kept sucking on his finger.

It seemed incredible: another life, born out of mine. If it's impossible to describe the thrill of a goal, just try and describe the birth of a son.

Of course we discovered that we were both ready for Maxi and we began to carry out our responsibilities, joyfully, day by day. When he cried, instead of rocking him in my arms, I would sit down in the big armchair, lay him on my chest and, while I was busy playing video games, he'd fall asleep.

When I was little, what made me happiest was to be able to have what other children had – to be able to wear something new and show it off – because I usually wore the same old tracksuit. I wore my football gear as everyday wear. If I needed a pair of socks, I'd put on a pair of long football socks. I'd try to hide them under my jeans, but everyone noticed at school and would make fun of me. I'd put on my older sister Sanela's tracksuits, and she was bigger than me. They'd hang on me like a sack and made me feel cool. Every day was a battle against poverty and shame.

My greatest happiness with my father was when he'd come and pick us up from my mother's place – me and my sister – because he was going to have us for the whole day. We'd go to a big car park, he'd sit me on his lap and I'd steer his navy-blue Opel Kadett while he held me. Then he'd take us out to eat enormous hamburgers and ice-cream with whipped cream on top. That was true happiness. We'd go fishing together frequently, too. One time I started fighting with Sanela and, as my father has a temper just like mine, he grabbed our fishing poles out of our hands and threw them into the sea: 'Time to go home.'

Today my mother is contented, and her happiness is part of mine. You can see in her face and her hands how hard she's worked all her life. She used to get up at four in the morning to go to work, and then she'd come home in the afternoon to take care of five children. She's had two Balkan husbands who drank too much and gave her more headaches than help.

When I got my first pay cheque from Ajax I told her, 'Mama, starting today, you never have to work again. I'll take care of you.'

And she replied, 'Zlatan, are you trying to kill me?'

'What do you mean?'

'If I stay home without working, it'll kill me. I need to stay busy.'

So we agreed that she could keep working, but shorter hours. No more than eight hours a day.

Now I've bought her an apartment in Croatia, near the island of Pag, where her two sisters live. She's very close to them, but for many years she never saw them, because of the war and everything else. As soon as Mama was fully vaccinated against Covid in Sweden, I put her on a plane and told her, 'Go and stay with your sisters, for as long as you want to. Your whole life you've taken care of other people, and now it's time to think about your own peace of mind. If we need something – or if you do – we'll come to you. And even if nobody needs anything, we'll come and see you anyway.'

I'm happy that she's comfortable there. She's content that way, and she's never asked me for anything. I want Maxi and Vincent to go and see her, all by themselves, without Mama and Papa. They need to learn to be independent. I want them to spend some time in Croatia with their grandmother, who has so much to teach them. Usually I go and see my father every time I return to Sweden. I go to Malmö from Stockholm and say hi to everyone. Otherwise, we almost never talk. My father isn't the kind of guy who's going to phone and discuss my matches. He used to do so; he'd always tell me where I'd made a mistake. He knew everything. He used to play when he was younger, but then he injured his knee and was forced to stop. At least that's what he told me, but I've actually never seen him on a football pitch.

Today when I travel to New York I fly first class, but the first time I visited I went with Helena, thanks to a pair of free tickets that we got with the points on her credit card. That was our first trip together and I remember it as a high point of happiness.

We didn't know anything about the city, so we took our inspiration from the hotel's brochures. We went to see the Statue of Liberty, and every night we'd go out to the movies. One day, as we wandered the city, we wound up on certain dark and sinister streets in Brooklyn. I got seriously worried.

'Helena, speed up and follow me.' I remember her struggling to keep up.

Our first years together were pure madness – sheer beautiful madness.

She arrived in Amsterdam only to discover that all I had in my apartment were a couple of plates, a glass and three pieces of cutlery. I was living like an animal.

Helena was older than me, more grown-up and more responsible. She taught me: 'You need to have at least twelve plates, twelve glasses, twelve of everything.' And she went out to buy them.

When I signed my contract with Juve, I suggested, 'Come and stay with me in Turin.'

And she looked at me and asked, 'Who do you think you are?' Helena had a career, as well as a house of her own in Sweden.

'Come on, you can come with me. Let's see if it works. We'll never know if we never try.'

'But I have a dog,' she tried to object.

'Do you absolutely have to bring the dog with you?'

'Yes.'

'Well then, bring the dog.'

As far as I'm concerned, she's the finest woman in the world. And she's with me.

Helena has the kind of energy that Gattuso has. Not only does she keep an eye on the kids' activities, but she also monitors all my business dealings and my investments. And every day she makes breakfast, lunch and dinner for our sons, takes them to training, keeps track of their work at school, takes the dogs out five times a day, washes the dishes and does the laundry.

Without a doubt, Maxi and Vincent could have no finer mother. It's only on Helena's account that I can live with such peace of mind in Italy, while my family is in Sweden. But she's already told me, 'When you're done playing football, I'm going to go back to work and you can take care of your boys all day, just like I've been doing all this time.'

Helena is tough. If she hadn't been, she would never have captivated me and she could never have lasted alongside me. Now that I'm forty, Zlatan Ibrahimović is a happy man. I have good health and everything else I could ever want. I lack nothing. I'm satisfied with what I've done and with what I'm doing now. I score fewer goals than I used to, and I don't chase after them with anything like the same frantic determination. That enables me to enjoy what I have, and the nice things that happen to me. Such as scoring a goal in a stadium that has filled back up with spectators, after the emptiness and silence of the pandemic.

Of all the things I possess, I could replace everything, except for two things: Maximilian and Vincent. They are my true happiness. Or really I should say: their happiness is my happiness. Our happiness. However much I might love cars, even the greatest automobile sooner or later starts to bore me and winds up in the back of the garage. True happiness isn't a moment, but is a sentiment that endures for ever. Like the way I feel about my sons.

There's only one thing that makes me anxious, and I've already told you about it: retiring from football. The closer I get to that time, the higher my anxiety climbs and the more incessant the question becomes: where will I find the adrenaline I need in order to live – the adrenaline that I've always taken from football?

But it's an anxiety that does nothing to undermine my happiness. In fact if anything, it's the opposite: if I already knew the future that awaits me, I'd certainly be less happy.

8. The Referee
(or *About the Law*)

At the beginning of my career, the referees were my worst enemies. I'd snarl at them, aggressive as a tiger in the arena, and they'd try to defend themselves with yellow and red cards. I was a bomb that would go off every time a whistle blew, feeling convinced that all referees had it in for me. It didn't help that I was big and strong and they mistook my strength for violence. I knew how to control balls with my feet two metres off the ground, with dizzying moves from Taekwondo. At that height, all I would encounter were other players' heads. And if I come into contact with shorter players, even without moving, I can hurt them badly. But it's not that I'm so violent; it's that they're so small.

Then someone explained to me that it's best to save your energy and not waste it on the referees, but instead to focus on the game. In the long run, I've learned.

After 800 or 900 matches, I've figured out that it does no good to argue with referees. If they've blown their whistle, they're not about to change their minds. I have two sons now, and I've matured; if I can, I try to help the referees. If I can do that and also help my team, so much the better. In any case, I do try and assist them.

Ever since I've come back to Italy I've noticed that the referees respect me and speak to me differently. Maybe that's because I've changed my attitude towards them. I give them a hand, and they don't keep their distance the way they used to. If anything, they explain what they're thinking and try to get me to help them solve on-field disputes.

Not all of them, though.

Parma–Milan, 10 April 2021: I take a couple of hard tackles from the defenders and I alert the referee. 'Hey, keep an eye out, boss.'

He says nothing.

Not long after that, the other team commits another ugly foul against Çalhanoğlu. Again I speak to the referee. 'Did you see that?'

No reaction.

So I tell him, 'If you're not interested in refereeing today, maybe you'd better go home.'

He replies, 'I'm not interested in anything you have to say.'

'Ah, you're not interested?' I retort. 'That strikes me as odd, you know.'

Instead of hearing 'odd', he thinks I said 'bastard' and kicks me off the field: red card. We're about twenty metres apart and he might very well have misunderstood me, or maybe he was waiting for this opportunity, just looking for a chance to make me pay.

It's an absurd sending-off. I try to walk over to him to ask for an explanation, but he hurries off in the opposite direction, literally running away. I go after him. 'Hold on . . .' Rebić stops me. So I give up trying to follow him, as I know it will only make things worse.

I leave the field and I swear to Pioli, 'Coach, when I mess up, I'm the first to admit it. You know that. But this time I didn't do a thing wrong. Nothing. Tonight you can watch the video and you'll see.' In fact in lots of the footage posted on YouTube, it's easy to read my lips: 'That strikes me as odd.'

I'm suspended for only one match, even though a straight red card is usually a three-match ban. But the assessment of a panel of top referees is that Enzo Maresca made a wrong decision.

However, I've lost out on a match and a half, and I have to hear the usual diatribe about what a bad boy Ibra is – how he's completely out of control. It's not true. I have the situation fully under control. What am I supposed to do if a referee gets it wrong? I hear what Italian pundit Billy Costacurta has to say about it: 'A leader can't afford to be kicked off the field and leave his team with just ten men.'

I send word to him, through a friend, 'You don't know me personally. So you need to shut up. Before you talk about me, get your facts straight: the referee made the mistake, I didn't. There was nothing I could have done to prevent that sending-off.'

At first I wanted to rip the referees limb from limb, but now I understand what a hard job they have, and the kind of pressures they're subjected to. I even realize that during our little training games at Milanello. My teammates always complain because they say that the referees are psychologically intimidated by me: 'Ibra's team always gets more penalties!'

That isn't true. In fact I'm often the one asking the referee not to let himself be intimidated by my presence, not to give me any get-out-of-jail-free cards, because I certainly don't need them.

If I were a referee, I'd be a good referee, because I have personality. I very much doubt I'd encounter a player who wouldn't respect and obey me. I'd let them play hard and I'd rarely use my whistle. I like seeing hard play, but that doesn't mean violent play. Only the most experienced referees can tell the difference.

One time I said that to the big boss of the referees, in a meeting at the start of the championship. 'You can't tell if I'm tackling someone to hurt them. You can freeze-frame the video and, based on the contact, you might judge an impact to have been violent, whereas if you look at the fluidity of the actual movement, it wasn't violent at all.'

On the other hand, a footballer can always tell if someone's tackling with the intention of hurting them. That's why I think it might be a good idea to let retired footballers serve as referees. I don't mean top-flight players, who necessarily have allegiance to this or that shirt, and whom the fans would automatically see as playing favourites; but the less famous, who might not have made it out of the minor leagues, but who still really understand the game. That way they, too, could finally make it onto the fields of the major stadiums, like the San Siro and Old Trafford.

I think that many referees were children with no talent for football, but still in love with it, who figured out this other way of being on a pitch with champions. Otherwise, why would you ever want to become a referee? What makes them do it?

Back in the days of my earliest experiences in Italy, I remember certain broadcasts where they'd argue about videotape replays for three or four hours on end. The poor referees were always being crucified. Things are better now. That is, except for the Video Assistant Referee monitors, which have created an unholy mess. Even now I don't understand how they work. Is the referee required to go to the side of the field to review the play if the VAR calls him, or not?

It's not only the referees who ask old Ibra for help in solving disputes on the pitch. His opponents do, too – Lazio manager Maurizio Sarri, for instance. I've turned into a bit of a football lawyer; I've gone over to the other side. Like the old-time *pistoleros* in westerns who put on a badge and become sheriffs.

Milan–Lazio, 12 September 2021: we're winning 2–0, I'm shielding the ball and, immediately after I pass to a teammate, Lucas Leiva tackles me hard from behind. I instinctively grab him by the throat, because I'm worried. I've just come back from four months out with a knee injury, and I don't want to get hurt again.

It's only for a second or two, though. I relax immediately and let go of him.

Francesco Acerbi shows up and starts acting tough. 'Do you want to hit me, too?'

'What the fuck are you talking about? Your friend is the

one who hit me,' I reply. 'Why don't you tell your team-mates to calm down, and then come back and talk to me.'

I'm relaxed, and in fact I laugh and kid around with their forward Pedro, and we hug. But all around us is sheer chaos.

Lazio's coach, Maurizio Sarri, comes over to me and bellows, 'Ibra, I'm sixty years old. That guy needs to show me respect! He can't be gesturing rudely at me like that!'

'Hey, sorry, I don't know what you're talking about. What happened? Who are you talking about?'

'Alexis Saelemaekers,' he replies, referring to our winger.

'What did he do to you?' I ask.

'He held up two fingers of one hand, like the number of goals Milan scored.'

'That's not right. Hold on, let me talk to him.'

I need to hear Alexis's version, too. I can't simply settle for one side of the story. Right or wrong, I always defend my teammates. Saelemaekers tells me that Sarri called him a 'piece-of-shit Frenchman', and he simply pointed to the scoreboard with the match score.

Neither thing is acceptable. We head into the tunnel leading to the dressing rooms.

The Lazio sporting director, Igli Tare, comes over. I'm on good terms with him. And so is their goalie, Pepe Reina, who wants to talk to Alexis.

I stop him. 'Listen, Pepe. Twenty of you have already attacked him. You're the twenty-first. You're a little late to the show. The kid understands. Now let me talk to your coach. He's the one who came looking for me.'

Reina retorts, 'Who do you think you are?'

Wrong question: one of the lines that really gets on my nerves.

'I don't think I'm anybody in particular. But what the fuck do you want, Reina?'

He calms down. Anyway I take Saelemaekers to talk to Sarri, so that they can work it out between them. They talk and Alexis apologizes. Peace reigns – it's all settled.

Sheriff Ibra, the new peace officer, has completed his mission.

March 2015, PSG–Lorient, 3–1: I score a hat-trick and, at the end of the match, I walk over to the referee so that he can give me the ball as a keepsake, as is traditional.

Tony Chapron, a football referee with the typical ego of a French player, who's since gone down in history for being banned after kicking a Nantes player during a match, cuts me dead. 'No.'

No? What do you mean? I scored three goals and I have a right to take the ball home with me. No way! I had to go to the kitman and get another ball. The 'hero' kept the actual ball from the match.

Some time later I found out that Chapron explained his decision in an interview with an English newspaper. 'I have four daughters, and if they don't ask politely, I don't even answer them. I did the same with Ibrahimović, who failed to show me manners and respect.'

Too bad that he didn't have the courage to say that while looking me in the eye. I'd have explained to Chapron that the right thing to do was to give me the ball and thank me, because refereeing me in a match was the greatest honour of his life. And I would have assured him that my two sons had better manners than his four daughters.

However, I have to say that French referees had their excuses, to give them their due: they had no experience, they weren't real professionals, they only reffed part-time and, above all, they weren't accustomed to interacting with real champions with major personalities. They weren't up to the level of football that Paris Saint-Germain had suddenly catapulted them into.

The same is true of American referees, who are a full-blown disaster. I even said so to their faces: 'You all need to go back to school and brush up on the basics.' Any time I even grazed someone, you'd have thought I'd sent them to the cemetery. Football isn't basketball – contact is allowed. They'd get it wrong, they'd be summoned over to the VAR and they'd refuse to go, out of sheer stubborn pride. Like the time a referee gave an absurd penalty and I asked him, 'What do you think you saw? Where were you anyway? On your coffee break?'

However, to return to France, we shouldn't forget what I'd said in Bordeaux because of a referee: that France was a piece-of-shit country. I could hardly expect them to give me special treatment.

At another championship match I'm having a drink at the edge of the field, and the fourth official comes over and tries to take the water bottle away from me. He just reaches out his arm to grab it, while I'm drinking from it. He tries once, twice, a third time. I'm forced to move and jab at him with my elbow to keep him from yanking the bottle out of my hand.

'What's wrong with you, man?' I'm thinking. 'My feet are outside the line, I'm not on the pitch. Beat it! Crazy. This kind of thing doesn't happen even at nursery school.'

I've never been refereed by a woman, as there aren't many female referees at this level. Maybe it would be better if they were lineswomen. But there are definitely some female referees on the pitch and they're good at their job. Leaving aside their skill levels and competence, they bring other benefits. You tend to control your reactions better in the presence of a woman. If you're the kind of person who'll blow up over a penalty, then in the presence of a female referee you're more likely to calm down. If you blow up anyway, that simply means you're a psychopath.

Still, if you want to work as a referee at a high level you need to be very solid mentally, and it doesn't matter if you're a man or a woman – the pressures out on the pitch are enormous. Players will shout in your face, surround you as they object and protest. If your mind isn't strong, then when you go home you'll be lucky if you don't wind up on the psychiatrist's couch.

At school I always obeyed schedules and rules, partly because my father was very strict. He didn't keep an eye on my studies or help me with my homework, but he demanded absolute discipline. My father was the law. He'd say, 'You need to be home by nine at night' and it never even occurred to me to miss that deadline.

He never raised his hands to me. Only once, when I seriously pushed him to the limit, did he lift me in the air over his head and throw me to the floor from six feet up. He had no need to beat me in order to demand obedience and respect. All he needed was his voice and that glare. He knew how to be aggressive, using stance and attitude alone. I never dared to contradict him, argue back or even challenge his decrees, because I was afraid of going too far and making a real mistake.

I was far less fearful of breaking other laws, though.

I've told the stories before: I stole bicycles and shoplifted enormous quantities of things from shopping malls. But that was different. It wasn't a challenge for its own sake; I was doing it to survive and to help myself feel equal to other kids of my age. I want a bicycle of my own. I can't have one? Well then, fuck it – I'll steal it. Too bad for the rightful owner, but I have to live, too, you know.

At school I'd see my classmates eating their morning snack. Papa never gave me money for a snack of my own. So I'd shoplift at the cafeteria. After all, I needed to eat.

Everyone wore Ralph Lauren and Tommy Hilfiger, but I wore the football gear I could steal from the Malmö club dressing room. That situation fenced me off, isolated me, made me feel different. It also made me mean, it's why I shoplifted, but none of it was easy.

One day I was with a friend of mine and we were caught stealing in a shopping mall. The police took us into the station and called our parents. Luckily my father wasn't home, or I wouldn't be around to tell the tale. It was my friend's father who came to get us. The police wrote a letter to my father to inform him of what had happened.

For days I kept an eye on the letterbox and, thank God, I managed to intercept it.

Like my father, I dictate law at home that is harsh and beyond appeal. When it comes to discipline, I'm as intransigent as my father was, but I speak to my sons far more than he ever did. I listen to their point of view and we compare notes. I make an effort to let them grasp the different angles on various situations.

It hasn't always been easy for my boys to bear my name and be compared to me. During our stay in England it was really difficult for Maxi at school, on more than one occasion. His classmates gave him a hard time because I'm his father. Maxi was even scolded by the headmaster and then punished at home. He's like his mother. He never asked me permission to play video games or play anything else, for that matter. He asked for my permission to read books. He asked *me*, who'd never read a single book in my life. He spent a whole week in his bedroom with the door closed, just reading.

My son.

I respect the law of training, and I respect the laws of my profession no less devoutly than I respected my father's rule of law.

It's pretty simple, really: there are twenty-five of us at Milan. How many other people in the world wish they could be in our place? Well then, that means we have to earn that privilege for ourselves, and recognize how lucky we are in every second of our daily training.

As I like to tell my teammates: 100 per cent is not

enough; you need to give 200 per cent in the work you do, because there's always someone else out there with the same dream you have, willing to die if that's what it takes to walk in your shoes. Given that fact, for the two hours you're going to spend in training, you'd better sweat hard and give the best you've got, because that forces everyone else to do the same and it helps the team grow. In that sense, Milan has improved enormously – in terms of mindset, in terms of working culture, we're ready now.

I am my own worst torturer, I assure you; the last person to cut myself a break.

I remember a training session shortly before I went back out onto the pitch against Lazio. It was an off-day, and every bone in my body ached with pain. I go to the person in charge of my recovery, a new expert recruited by Juve who works in the delicate intermediate area between recovery from an injury and return to a group.

'Listen, I'm going to be straight with you: I'm not at my best today and I really don't feel like training at all. Don't worry, though. You tell me what I need to do and, when we get started, I'll give you a thousand per cent, the way I always do.'

I always like to know the work plan, down to the smallest details, before getting started. That way I can programme myself, free my mind of thoughts and then I will plough through all the way to the last exercise.

I don't like it when people tell me, 'Let's get started and then we can see how you feel.' No, let's not see a darned thing. The way I *feel* doesn't matter. All that matters is what

I'm supposed to do. I'll do it, right down to the last detail, no matter what happens.

But when it comes to traffic regulations and speeding laws, I'm much less of a stickler. As I said earlier, jamming my foot down on the accelerator and roaring off on the motorway is a form of freedom for me. I'm not comfortable being surrounded by so many people. I'm uneasy because I know they all know who I am, and I feel like a monkey behind bars in the zoo. The car gives me a way to escape.

Over the years I've put together a very nice collection of speeding tickets. Less so in Italy because, if I'm in luck and the traffic cop is an AC Milan fan, usually all it takes is an autograph or selfie . . .

Even though I need the option to escape in order to feel free, I always do it in a responsible manner. I never drive fast on roads jammed with traffic – never in the city. I drive fast on the motorway, and only when the coast is clear and it's safe. I never put other drivers and passengers at risk.

One day I was doing some shopping near my house and I lost track of the time. I had to be at lunch in Milanello at 1 p.m. It takes at least fifty minutes to get there. I'm never going to make it.

I call the team manager and explain that I've been in a collision and I'll be showing up a little late. I tell the physio, 'I'll drive.'

I leave my house at 12.17 and at 12.58 I'm sitting at the table in Milanello – timely as hell. A new world record for the route from Porta Nuova to Carnago.

*

People often ask me, 'So, at Juve, didn't you ever notice that the referees had suddenly become much friendlier?'

I reply, 'No. On the pitch all I ever noticed is that we were playing better. And that's why we won.'

I was still young and, as far as I was concerned, the referee was my enemy. Eleven of us, twelve of them. I could never manage to think of referees as being on my side.

I gave a speech at a music festival and was given some notes to use. I was so focused that I didn't even notice the mistake. They had me say that I'd won the Scudetto eleven times when, in fact, the correct number was thirteen. UEFA and Federcalcio, the Italian Football Federation, don't count the two Scudetti stripped from Juve in the aftermath of the Calciopoli match-fixing scandal.* But I'll always consider them to have been personal victories, 100 per cent. If I hadn't missed it, I'd have said thirteen, not eleven.

When I walk into the Turin stadium and see the number thirty-eight next to the tricolour Scudetto, I don't think of it as a mistake – I think it's exactly the right number, and that its presence there represents true justice: we won both those Scudetto titles because we were the best team in Italy, but then they took them away from us.

I don't know whether the system was manipulated in

* In May 2006 intercepted phone calls revealed the relations between managers and referee organizations during the 2004–5 and 2005–6 seasons and there were accusations of favourable referees being selected.

any way, and I don't care to ask. That's a choice I've made; I decided from the very outset to ignore the investigation and the controversy. All I know for sure is that no one ever manipulated the way I ran on the pitch – none of my goals, the hard work I put in in training, my injuries, my accidents and my pain. No one manipulated the sweat and talent of my teammates. After seventy or eighty matches, only the strongest team wins: it's the justice of the pitch that matters in sport. That's why I'll go on thinking of the two Scudetti they stripped us of as being rightfully mine. How was it even conceivable to give one of the two Scudetti to someone else? And how could that someone else bring themselves to accept it?

If you disqualify the team that won it and then you give me their medal, I don't want it. In fact I consider it an insult if you try to give it to me at all. If I walk around with that medal hanging from my neck and I say, 'I won!' it merely strikes me as pathetic.

I've always had a very good relationship with Luciano Moggi, the executive at the centre of the scandal, and that's partly because he behaved differently with foreigners: he laughed, he joked around, he made wisecracks . . . Whereas the Italians were all afraid of him.

Whenever Moggi entered the dressing room, it was like when Berlusconi arrived in Milanello: you could feel the vibrations in the air, the sheer weight of his charisma; everyone fell silent, fearful and intimidated.

But I was young, and I never felt overwhelmed, I just called him 'boss'. He had a good relationship with Mino, and that helped us to bond. Moggi did a lot for me, even if he did stick me with a few too many fines. Like that time with Jonathan Zebina.

I should tell you that, in Italy, players can have their salary docked on the basis of unwritten rules, such as showing up late or behaving disrespectfully. This was an in-house training match. Zebina tackled me hard from behind, once, twice, three times.

I don't like being tackled from behind like that, because I can't see it coming. I'm not expecting it, especially in training, and there's a serious risk of injury. But if I know that a defender in a practice game means to tackle me roughly, like in a real match, then I get ready when the ball comes my way. So I turn round and tell Zebina, 'If you want to play rough, say so and I'll know you're coming.'

He gives me a head-butt, so I let fly with a right and deck him.

Lilian Thuram reaches us and shoves me away. 'What an idiot you are, Ibra! What an idiot!'

Cannavaro rushes up, pushes Thuram aside and tells me, 'You've done it this time, Zlatan!' But even as he's saying it, he gives me a wink.

Capello, the coach, is on the far side of the field, leaning against a pole. He shouts, 'Lilian! Lilian!'

Whenever Capello shouted, absolute silence would fall.

'Lilian! Get out of there. Leave him alone.' Thuram moves away and the storm subsides.

After training, I go and talk to Capello: 'I'm sorry, Coach.'

'About what?' he asks.

'That incident with Zebina.'

'No need to apologize. That kind of thing does the team good,' he replied.

I go and get a massage, a shower and all the rest. After three hours Zebina still has an ice-bag on his eye. The manager, Alessio Secco, alerts me: 'You're being asked for.' If Moggi wanted to see you, that's how you found out – you were told, 'You're being asked for.' No one even said his name. Everybody understood.

If, for instance, some player was refusing to give an interview and Secco told him, 'You're being asked for', then that player knew he'd be giving the interview in question, because that's the way Moggi wanted it.

I go to Moggi's office, and he tells me, 'Zlatan, I have to fine you.'

'Why?'

'The fight with Zebina.'

'No, I'm not paying.'

'Oh, you'll pay all right.'

'Listen, boss. If someone attacks you on the street, what do you do?' I ask him.

'I defend myself,' he replies.

'I defended myself when Zebina attacked me,' I explain.

'Okay, but you were wrong. Just pay the fine and we're done.'

I read the amount of the fine. 'This is way too much. I mean, I didn't kill the guy!'

'Don't worry, he'll be paying a fine, too,' Moggi reassures me.

'How big a fine?'

'Ten times the amount of your fine,' Moggi replies.

'All right then – in that case, I'm good with it. Maybe you could simply roll my fine into his and make him pay it all.'

One day we arrive at the stadium. I'm expecting to play, but they inform me that I should go to the stand. Not even on the bench: in the stand.

'What's going on?' Nobody can give me an explanation.

I call Mino. 'Mino, I was supposed to be playing today, and instead I've been sent to the stand without an explanation. Try and see what you can find out.'

Alessio Secco shows up. 'Zlatan, tomorrow you're being asked to see Moggi.'

The next day Moggi explains. 'The reason you didn't play yesterday is that you used some kind of cream and failed to inform us.'

'Wait, what does that have to do with football? I'm having problems with psoriasis on my arms,' I explain. 'It's a cream they gave me when I was at Ajax.'

'It's got cortisone in it. You're obliged to tell us everything you take. We need to know everything – literally everything. This is going to cost you another fat fine,' the boss decrees.

I read the sum and, once again, I'm stunned. 'For some stupid skin cream?'

'Do it again and the fine will double.'

Maybe I should have kept the psoriasis.

At Juve, they were especially sensitive about pharmaceuticals of any kind, because Dr Riccardo Agricola's doping trial was under way. If they had happened to find any trace of a forbidden substance in my anti-doping tests, it would have meant a devastating blowback in terms of the club's image.

That's just the way Moggi was: extremely harsh. When he had something important to say to the team, he summoned us all to the gym. Not the dressing room or the pitch: the gym. We'd gather round in a circle and he'd stand in the middle. Only he was allowed to talk.

I remember a day when he attacked one of my teammates in front of everyone. Moggi accused him of being unproductive and threatened to dock half his salary. The young man tried to have his say, but his boss shut him up fast: 'Not a word or it'll cost you two months' pay.'

Moggi was relentless, but I like people like that – people who are clear and concise: it's black or white. No muddling around with shades of grey.

After the refereeing scandal of 2006, Juve was relegated to Serie B. I chose to leave the club and join Inter, Moggi's worst enemy. When I informed him of the fact, he didn't utter a word of criticism. In fact he said nothing at all, partly because at the time he had far more serious problems on his hands.

I started my preparation in the mountains. I was sharing a room with Pavel Nedvěd, but I was waiting to leave. If I'd been the age I am now, I would have stayed to help the team climb back up into Serie A, the way I did with Milan, which I did so much to elevate. But I was at the start of my career, and I wanted to play in the Champions League, not in Serie B. In short, I was young and hungry for achievement.

Before I signed for Inter, AC Milan had made me an offer too, and the contract they'd proposed was a good one, but there was a condition: I'd have to wait for the qualifying round of the Champions League against Red Star Belgrade. 'If we qualify, the club will have more money.'

AC were confident I'd come play for them, no matter what happened, because it was one of the most fashionable clubs. It had only been three years since they'd won the Champions League, while Inter hadn't won the Scudetto in seventeen years.

But Inter made me a better offer. So Mino went back to AC Milan and said, 'If Ibra is going to be your number-one footballer, then he needs to have the team's highest salary.'

Ariedo Braida and Galliani replied, 'Not even if the Virgin Mary appears to us in a vision will we so much as touch the contract we just offered you.'

I took the answer invoking the Virgin Mary as an insult. It meant that AC Milan didn't want me badly enough, and I'm not going anywhere that I sense a shortage of enthusiasm.

I told Mino, 'Make the deal with Inter. I'll bring them the Scudetto again, after a seventeen-year drought. That's the challenge.'

The evening that I signed for Inter, Berlusconi was out to dinner at Da Giannino, a Milan restaurant. He was playing the guitar with a tableful of friends. They were all laughing and having a good time. I've been told that the minute someone told him I'd signed for Inter, he put down his guitar and sat in silence for an hour.

9. The Injury
(*or About Pain*)

My left hand is different from my right hand. You can see a bone jutting out. It happened in the summer of 2009. I was touring with Inter in America. During a match against Chelsea I was involved in a tough tackle with John Terry and I came out of it with a sharp, persistent pain in my left hand that wouldn't go away.

Before my transfer to Barcelona in August of that same year I went in and explained to the doctor, 'I think there's something wrong with this hand.' So they found a fracture at the base of my second metacarpal. They operated immediately and stabilized it with two screws.

At Paris Saint-Germain I was out of action for forty-five days because of a mysterious injury. I can't be sure, of course, but I'm convinced that someone punched a hole in a tendon with a hypodermic needle during an ankle treatment. They always denied it, but the tests I had done in Sweden found a hole that was probably caused by the injection.

And then the worst injury of all – a terrible one, when I was at Manchester United – kept me off the pitch for seven months and changed my life.

Europa League, Manchester United–Anderlecht, 20 April 2017: there are thirty seconds left till the end of the match. I'm tired. Very tired. It's nearly the end of the season. Mourinho had me play every single match, and that's partly because I never asked a coach to let me rest. I wanted to be there for every single battle.

I leap up into an aerial duel with a defender, but then, when I return to earth, I must have miscalculated my time to touchdown. I thought I'd jumped higher. I hadn't expected to hit the grass that fast. My knee, completely out of control, makes an unnatural movement backwards and to the side. It's bent in a way it never should be. More than the pain, I feel a strange sensation, as if I've swallowed my tongue. I'm filled with adrenaline.

I tell myself, 'It's nothing. I'm Superman.' I try to get back up on my feet, but something's wrong. I lack strength, and I have no sense of balance. I try again. It's no good. The Man U doctors come running; they touch my knee and immediately signal for a substitution.

Okay, I leave the pitch. After all, the match is over; but no stretcher and no one helping me, thank you very much. I want to walk off on my own two feet because, in my mind, I'm fine. Nothing serious has happened. I leave the crowded stadium. But back in the dressing room, my physio Dario checks me over and, without a word, shakes his head sadly. Then it starts to dawn on me that the situation isn't great.

All the same, my ego refuses to give up the fight. I decline to put on a knee brace to leave the stadium, and I also refuse to take the pain medication they prescribe for me. I stick the pills in my pocket. I'm Superman.

When I get home I head for the bathroom. I try to

stand up from the toilet, but I can't do it. My flexor muscle has given out. Since I was injured, this is the first time I've bent my leg at a ninety-degree angle. I feel a horrible jolt of pain.

I call Helena, shouting, 'Come here! Come here!'

She pulls my leg to get me back into an upright position. I relax a little, but the pain has only worsened. This time no doubt about it: Superman is going to down handfuls of painkillers.

In the morning I get out of bed, I stand in front of a mirror and I take a picture of my knees to compare them. The right knee is much bigger than the left one, without any sharp definition – completely round – and the pain is intolerable.

I go to training without a knee brace. In my mind, I'm still convinced that whatever has happened, it's nothing especially serious. It's just a sprain or something like that. It'll pass. Swelling is normal in cases like these. Instead, the MRI results are a punch to the face: tear of the cruciate ligament, the external collateral ligament, and a detached biceps femoris tendon. Everything's a wreck. I clutch at hope and ask for a second opinion.

Even before we can get a definitive diagnosis and announce it, Mino's mobile starts popping: surgeons offering to operate on me. A flock of vultures. Mino dresses down a renowned surgeon from Rome who's worked on lots of football stars: 'What are you saying you'd operate on, if we don't even know what's wrong with that knee? How dare you call me up like this? Go look for publicity somewhere else!'

Yes, I have to admit that Mino used far more colourful language than that.

I ask Dario, 'Tell me the names of the first three surgeons you'd talk to.'

We go to ten people that we trust and ask exactly the same question. Everyone gives us the same name first: Freddie Fu, an American doctor who comes from Hong Kong. At the same time, everyone warns us that it'll be impossible to get an appointment with him because he's always too busy. He's a world-renowned authority, and he's received all kinds of prestigious awards. I google him and there's a picture of him with Barack Obama. The city of Pittsburgh, in recognition of the work he's done, has even dedicated a day of the year to him, as if he were some kind of saint: 13 September. Every 13 September is celebrated as 'Dr Freddie Fu Day'.

I report back to Mino, who alerts me a few days later, 'Pack your bags. Tomorrow we're going to Pittsburgh. I've already made the reservations. Freddie Fu is expecting us.' Mino isn't exactly a saint, but he does know how to perform some real miracles.

We land in the States in the early hours of the morning: me, Mino and Dario. We don't even go to the hotel; instead we drive straight to UPMC, the University of Pittsburgh Medical Center, and there we are greeted by – standing in an impressive array in front of the main entrance – Freddie Fu in person, his right-hand man Dr Volker Musahl and six other doctors.

At 4 a.m.

They perform all sorts of exams on me: MRIs,

sonograms and all the rest. And then Freddie Fu tells us, 'Come back at seven a.m. and we'll talk it over.'

A short stay in the hotel and then we're back in the hospital. They usher us into a big room, darken all the windows and project a series of pictures: the dynamics of the injury in Manchester, the damage suffered; all the measurements and other data concerning my knee; the results of the exams done three hours earlier; and a simulation of the operation they intend to carry out.

In all my previous visits to other doctors they had explained that I'd have to undergo two operations: a first one for the cruciate ligament and a second one, a few months later, for the external ligament and the damaged muscle.

It would have taken too much time. Now I was looking for a surgeon who could do it all in one go.

Freddie Fu reassured me, 'No problem. I only need to go in once.'

Mino looks over at me. 'What do you think?'

'That what I've seen gives me all the confidence I need,' I reply.

'All right then, we'll stay here,' Mino decides.

'The swelling in the knee needs to go down. I'll be able to operate in a week,' the great surgeon concludes.

Okay. We go out to see the city of Pittsburgh. A couple of days later Mino receives a phone call from the surgeon. 'Get ready, because I'll come and pick up Zlatan at four in the morning.'

'But the operation was supposed to take place next week, wasn't it?'

'No, I just had a dream and I saw that I need to do the operation tomorrow,' Freddie Fu explains. He's a strange guy, but then so are all geniuses. When he talks, it always seems as if he's performing in a theatre: he gesticulates, he takes long pauses, he quotes poetry by heart, he tells stories that sound really weird and unlikely. Like his story about the chimpanzee.

He explained that his medical centre was doing experimental surgery on animals, trying out new techniques to repair cruciate ligaments. He gave us the example of a chimpanzee that was having knee problems.

'How did they know he was having problems?' I asked.

'Because he stopped having sex,' Freddie Fu replied. 'Before that, he was having sex three times a day.'

'And was the operation successful?'

'Yes, to the delight of the chimp's girlfriend.'

'Great,' I commented. 'If you've already had a chance to practise on animals, then you should have no problems with me.'

Freddie Fu doesn't send an ambulance or one of his assistants to pick me up from the hotel. He comes to get me in person, at four in the morning. My first thought is this: 'If he operates anything like the way he drives, I'd better start worrying.'

He comes close to running off the road at one point.

I warn him at the last second. 'Hey, Freddie Fu!'

He jerks the wheel and yanks the car back onto the tarmac. This happens twice.

'Everything all right, Doc? You okay?' I ask him.

'Everything's fine. Don't worry.'

I'm not that thrilled to be told I shouldn't worry. I mean, in a few hours' time this man is going to be operating on me.

The fact is that Freddie Fu is always busy thinking, his brain works all the time and he's always in a world of his own. But maybe it would be better if he could avoid doing it while driving, or in the operating theatre.

I glance over at Mino in some alarm and he tells me: 'Calm down, calm down . . .' That's what he always says: 'Calm down, calm down.'

We get to the hospital. Everything's ready for the operation. Freddie Fu picks up a felt-tip pen and writes something on my knee.

'What's that?' I ask.

'My signature in Chinese.'

'And why'd you do it?'

'To make sure I cut into the correct knee. You know, on my first thousand operations I almost always got them wrong. After that I improved,' he tells me with a wink.

They put me under and the operation begins. It lasts for two hours and forty-five minutes.

They told me that my knee seemed like the knee of a young man, strong and solid, because up till then it had never been injured. And that the ligament they used, to extract a portion of tissue to repair the damaged one, was so big that I wouldn't lose so much as an ounce of strength. Instead of two or three screws, the normal number, they implanted six in me. It's impossible to think that it could ever tear again.

In other words, the operation was a complete success.

I'm eager to go straight back to the hotel because, as I've already said, I have a hard time breathing in hospital. I want to leave, but I can't keep my eyes open on account of the anaesthesia. I open and shut my eyes, over and over again. I seem like a mobile phone with a faulty battery. I spend the whole day like that, and then finally, towards evening, I manage to wake up entirely and we leave the hospital. That's when the real hell begins.

For two weeks I have to remain motionless in bed – I can't place any strain at all on my leg. It's real torture. I'm not used to lying still. At the very most, I might do so during my few weeks of summer holiday. This injury has come when I was in top condition, when all my body wants to do is run, work hard and fight. Instead I'm being asked to lie motionless. I feel as if I've been buried alive.

Mino realizes what's going on and makes a decision. 'We need to get out of here. Let's go take a walk.'

They give me a pair of crutches, the kind that fit under your armpits, but they hurt me. I try a pair of the shorter kind, the ones where you grab the handle. They aren't much better.

'Listen, Dario, why don't you push me around for a while in a wheelchair.'

My physio refuses. 'No, the world can't see you in a wheelchair.'

This is the first time I've been out of bed since the operation. Mino takes me to the gym to see if I can build up a little strength. But we leave before long, because I'm not feeling great.

'I'm going back to my room,' I announce and, right in front of the lift, I fall flat on the floor. Out cold.

A drop in blood sugar. I'm as white as a ghost. Mino gives me some jelly to eat. He's spoon-feeding me, as if I were a child. On the third day I've been dragging myself around on my crutches, struggling up the stairs, stumbling over manholes in the street and bumping into revolving doors. I just throw the pair of crutches at Dario, insulting him in every language I know. I'm a hysterical zombie because my whole world has suddenly collapsed.

I can no longer play, run, fight or experience the adrenaline I'm so addicted to. Now I'm going to have to wait a year. I'm starting to realize what that means.

All I can do in the first few weeks is contract and relax the muscle to build up some tone and reactivate the connection between my brain and my leg. It's a form of mental practice, performed while lying on my back. I clench the muscle and release it, clench and release it, at a steady pace: 2,000 times in three hours.

After two weeks we start doing leg-bending exercises. I have to succeed in flexing it as much as possible during the first two months, because after that it may not get any better. In such cases you tend to remain at the level of mobility that you regain in the first sixty days. I have to force it, but not too much, to avoid excessive strain on the external ligament.

When Dario manipulates my leg, I shout in agony. Every single day Mino brings me food. He takes care of everything, as usual, but at a certain point he can't stand being locked inside any more, either. 'Zlatan, I'm sick of Pittsburgh. Let Freddie Fu know that we're going to go and work in Miami and we'll continue your rehabilitation there.'

The surgeon okays this plan and we stay in Miami for a week, then we go back to Sweden to continue the recovery exercises. You know the rest of the story: the workout machines in my gym, the return to Manchester, the mistake due to Mourinho's people's excessive haste, the decision to go to America . . . I was thirty-five when I had the operation.

There were lots of people who thought I'd reached the end of the line. Actually, though, right after the operation, Freddie Fu promised the journalists, 'Ibrahimović's career is anything but over. He'll be playing for a long time to come.'

He was right. He totally deserved and earned it: the day named after him on the calendar.

After the injury I suffered during the Juve–Milan match on 9 May 2021, Dr Volker Musahl, Fu's right-hand man, flew to Milanello for an examination. A sprain of my other, left knee this time. He recommended a cautious course of therapy, but the pain wouldn't stop and so Volker came back to Italy and operated on me arthroscopically in the Roman branch of the UPMC.

Then I lower my head and go back to work like an animal, with the pain that I delight in and the usual conviction in my brain: it's nothing – I'll soon be better and stronger than ever.

In fact when I return to the team four months later, the results of my tests are the best of anyone's. I'm in better shape than my teammates who have got two months of training in their legs. Even Pioli is surprised, almost frightened. 'It's not normal for you to be in such good shape.'

I go back out onto the pitch against Lazio and I immediately score that goal wearing the samurai plait.

Pioli and I come up with a gradual recovery plan: half an hour with Lazio; first-choice player at Anfield against Liverpool; and then we'll see how I do in those two matches and we can decide how long to let me play against Juventus.

Instead I stop playing again because of tendinitis, and that's when I realize it's not going well at all. I need to change something. For the first time in my life I come to terms with the fact that I'm not immortal. I've become a human being.

I forced things far too much in the previous months, to prove that I was up to my teammates' level, at my advanced age of thirty-nine. And that steered me into a string of injuries: muscle problems and other issues like that. I kept falling out of the team and scrambling back in. I'd leave and then return. My body was sending me a series of messages that I would promptly ignore. The time had come to listen to what it had to say and to change my approach to the injuries, just as I modified my style of play.

I can no longer afford one sprint after another, lunge after lunge on the attack, the way I did when I was a youngster. Now I need to conserve my strength. And I can no longer fight for ninety minutes in the penalty area, where bodies are flying in all directions and it's easy to get hurt. I'm staying out of the fray more. I have so many years of experience under my belt that I only go in when I can do some good, working harder for other players' goals than for my own. I've become a new, very different player, with the changes that I've made to meet the demands of my ageing body.

Likewise, I've had to change the way I deal with injuries. I can't go on saying to myself: 'It's nothing, I'll be back stronger than ever.' Today it takes me longer to recover from the effort of a match, and longer to cope with a blow or a sprain. I have to work much harder than before. After team training every day I add a series of individual exercises that are custom-tailored for me.

After the age of thirty I started to pay closer attention to my diet. Nothing extreme, but I have eliminated certain foods and drinks: I no longer eat pasta twice a day, and if I eat meat at lunch, I avoid it at dinner. And I always make sure that I have a substantial breakfast to start the day right.

If I'm still playing at the highest levels at the age of forty, it's not because of divine grace or any gift of nature; it's because I've worked hard and made enormous sacrifices. Now that I clearly understand I'm no longer Superman, I pick my battles, and I've decided two things.

First of all: I'm not running any more pointless risks. I'm going back to training, followed by actual play in matches, only when I feel absolutely ready. I need a new type of discipline and a great fund of patience.

Second: now that my body is more exposed to injury,

it's going to be fundamental to have a personal physio who really knows that body well and can keep an eye on it 24/7/365. A sentinel standing guard over my health.

That's why I've hired Giorgio. He has many years of experience, he's considered to be one of the best and he works for me, and me alone. He taught Dario, who's now at Paris Saint-Germain, but who previously worked at Inter. When I renewed my contract with Milan, Inter let him go.

Dario did a fantastic job of restoring stability to my knee after the operation. I'm not having any further trouble with it, and it's working perfectly. Unfortunately, inflammation then started in the tendon, which has absolutely nothing to do with the knee. It's on account of an injection given some time back when I was at PSG. The scar revived and created a haematoma. The inflammation derived from the introduction of blood and fluid.

I started feeling pain in my left tendon the week before the Lazio match, during my trial game against the under-nineteen Primavera team, but I paid it no attention. 'It's probably a really hard pitch,' I thought.

We have a new pitch at Milanello. It's very nice, but the ground seemed too hard to me, right from the start. At first I thought: 'I just need to get used to it.' I wasn't thinking very much about the tendon, because I was so focused on the knee, and the knee was better.

I'd taken the time to heal with full awareness of one thing: 'When I get back to the game, I'm going to strike fear into hearts.'

The tests and the pitch indicated that I was in top condition, that I was stronger than anyone else on the team. Then, during the Milan–Lazio match, Tiémoué Bakayoko comes onto the pitch from the bench and, after a few minutes, gets injured.

I walk over to him and ask, 'Hey, Baka, is it your tendon?'

He replies: 'Yes.'

'Did it hurt already before the match?'

'Yes.'

Me, Baka and a third player: all of us with aching tendons. So it was the new pitch. I'm scared now: if I get injured too, right after returning to the team following a four-month recuperation, what is everyone going to think? That I'm an old man, ready for the rubbish dump.

I scored a goal against Lazio. I backed up a few metres and started playing as simply as I could, avoiding all risks. The next day at Milanello I still felt a little pain, but we only did some light exercise.

On the eve of the Milan–Liverpool match I tried to force myself during the tactical exercises: five or six sharp sprints. No problem for the first three. On the fourth one I started to feel some pain. On the fifth, it got a little worse. After the sixth sprint, I couldn't move with the rest of the team: they'd run and I'd walk. When they moved up in defence, I was still back in the midfield. Instead of running on my toes, I was ambling along on the backs of my heels to limit the pain.

I told Pioli, 'Coach, if I'm like this tomorrow in Liverpool, you need to take me off after fifteen minutes.'

'I'm taking you off now, Zlatan.'

On this occasion I took all the time I needed to get back in shape. I wasn't twenty years old any more. Not physically, anyway. In my head, I was the same as I always was.

I don't want to think about what I'll look like when I'm old, and how my tattoos will age with the rest of me. I made sure to have them done on my back, so that I didn't have to see them. I have no tattoos on my legs. There are only the scars from my old playing style, and from my history as a football player. On my wrist I've tattooed my brother Sapko's date of birth: 30 April 1973. He was forty-one when he died.

Leukaemia carried him off in fourteen months. That's why I don't want to think about the future and why I'm focused strictly on the present. I try not to waste so much as a second and to be as close as possible to my boys, and to share my time with them and the people I love, because I know that life flies by, and all it takes is a visit to the doctor to turn everything upside down.

When I asked Sapko how he realized he was sick, he told me that he was walking down the street and suddenly felt a strange sensation, as if he were drowning on the pavement. It was as if he was underwater and couldn't breathe. He went straight to the hospital and took a series of tests. They didn't tell him a thing. The next day the doctor called Papa and gave him the news.

'How bad is this leukaemia?' I asked him.

'Aggressive,' was what Papa told me.

'But we're stronger than it is. We'll win this battle, too.'

Sapko started the treatment, but in a few months his condition had grown worse. I came home from Paris, where I was playing, and found a brother who was all swollen up, without hair, and who was already having difficulty moving.

It was extremely tough to see him in that state. I wasn't ready for it. He'd had to take lots of pills that made him feel a little better, but only for a short time. Papa helped him get to the bathroom and then came back to the living room, where he admitted to me, for the first time, 'There's no hope.'

I looked at him and realized how serious it was. It was spelled out clearly in his eyes. I couldn't breathe. I couldn't swallow. How could this be? Sapko was giving me hope, and Papa was taking it away.

With all the strength I had in my body, with all the money in my bank account, with all the friends and contacts I had around the world, I still couldn't do a thing to help my brother. I felt totally powerless, an absolute zero.

I was a wreck.

To go on playing was a real torment, even though, with the force of my will and my sense of responsibility, I was able to programme myself: for ninety minutes I focused solely on the pitch, giving my all to my profession, and only after did I remember my pain.

Sapko was doing even worse. We took him to a hospice for the terminally ill, but he stayed there for only a week. He didn't like it. So Papa decided, 'I'll take him back to my house.'

But by now Papa was exhausted from the grief and

effort he'd put into caring for his son, twenty-four hours a day for more than a year. He hadn't left Sapko's side for so much as a minute. He'd grown weaker himself and could no longer lift his son up, even though by now Sapko was as light as a feather. Papa was forced to take him back to the clinic.

We're eliminated by Chelsea in the Champions League and I tell my coach, Laurent Blanc, 'Coach, I'm going back to Sweden. I want to be near my brother.'

At that time we still have the pink house in Malmö, and my whole family is there. My flight from Paris arrives late in the evening. The next morning I get up and eat breakfast. I'm in no hurry – I feel as if I have all the time in the world. I go out, forget my jacket and have to go back. I get in the car and head over to the clinic, but then I can't find it.

I call Papa, who steps outside and meets me, and together we go up to Sapko's room.

He's already in a coma. His breathing is rough and irregular.

Papa explains to me that the pauses between breaths are getting longer. He's sitting at the foot of the bed, next to a window. I'm standing beside him, but I'm having a hard time looking at my brother. I can't do it. I just listen to each breath drawing out, longer and longer.

After ten minutes Papa says, 'There, it's over.'

'What?'

'He's not breathing any more.'

Sapko waited for me before dying. He wanted me there, beside him. I'm absolutely certain of that fact. I'd slept in, had an unhurried breakfast and taken my time. But he waited for me. Only once I got there, did my brother take his last breath.

Papa stands up to cover Sapko's face with the sheet, but I stop him. 'No, don't touch him. Let someone else do it.'

The funeral was held according to the Muslim rite. The simple coffin was handed from relative to relative, from friend to friend. Those who'd carried it went back to the end of the queue to carry it again. It's a chain of human arms accompanying the deceased to the grave. The six people closest to him, chosen by Papa, took care of lowering the coffin into the grave on cloth straps.

Beside the grave, where many people gathered to take part in the ceremony, there were stacks of shovels. Papa took one and tossed the first shovelful of dirt onto the coffin. Then it was my turn, and I did the same, once, twice, and then I couldn't go on. I dropped the shovel. Covering my brother up with dirt would have meant accepting his death, whereas in my mind Sapko was still alive. I couldn't accept that he was no longer with us. He was too young, he was my brother. I went back to my family and I wept with them.

Papa never shed a tear. The next day he returned to the cemetery, alone, and wept all day, from morning to evening. He explained, 'I'll do it once, then never again.'

When I heard the news about the Bologna manager – 'Mihajlović has leukaemia' – I was plunged back into the nightmare of Sapko, I relived those awful days. I wanted to call Siniša immediately, but I didn't have the strength to do so.

After a few days I was able to do it. I was in Los Angeles and I calculated the right time to call him, taking into account the nine hours' time difference. 'If I call him late at night, when it's early morning for him, that might be best, because in the evening he'll be tired,' I figured.

I call him, but I don't really know what to say. 'How are you?' The guy has leukaemia and you ask him, 'How are you?' It's a stupid question.

Siniša realizes I'm stammering and having a hard time talking, so he goes ahead and does the talking for me. '*Bato* . . .' he says.

That's what Siniša calls me. *Bato*, in Serbian, means 'son of mine'.

'*Bato*, you know me. You know that I'll win this battle. I'm too strong – I'm okay. Don't worry.' He's the one who is comforting and encouraging me.

I don't know much about leukaemia. I only had the one devastating experience of it with my brother. As Mihajlović talks to me, I wonder if this will be my last conversation with him and whether I've already seen him for the last time.

Right in the middle of my fever of doubts and fears, he says to me, 'I need an attacker. Come and play for us.'

You understand? Siniša took it for granted that he'd get better, he was already past the disease, he was already sitting in the Bologna dugout and he was waiting for me.

'Siniša, I'm thinking about quitting entirely. I'm an old man, I can't run any more.'

'I don't need you to run. I just need you to score goals. We have other guys who'll do the running for you.'

Marco Di Vaio, chief executive of Bologna, came to Los Angeles to talk it over with me. I told him, 'Look, it's pointless talking to me about stadiums, fans, history or whatever else, to convince me. If I'm coming to Bologna, I'm only doing it for Mihajlović.'

Siniša was a powerful motivator, but I couldn't be sure I'd see him in the dugout again, and Bologna as a team wasn't giving me the charge of adrenaline that I needed. And then, as I told you, Napoli and Milan showed up.

I called Siniša. 'You're the first one I'm telling. No one else knows it yet: I'm going to Milan. I'm sorry.'

He answered me, 'You did the right thing. A smart decision.'

We saw each other again on the pitch at the San Siro. This was when Mihajlović was still checking in and out of hospital. He'd only leave the hospital to sit in the dugout, as he wanted to be there. With his little cap and his mask. Before a match I never say hello to the opposing coaches, even if I know them well, like Mourinho. But I insisted on hugging Siniša, and if anybody had tried to stop me, they wouldn't have been able to. What I wanted was to give him a moment of joy and energy, just as he'd done for me so many times.

Pioli told me about the cancer that hit Ivan Gazidis, Milan's chief executive officer. We exchange texts. In his last text, Gazidis told me, 'Go on leading Milan the way you're doing.'

'It's a promise,' I wrote back.

I'm convinced that the good and evil that a person has done on this Earth come back to them, and that the circle is unbroken – but here, on Earth. I don't believe in a second life. When you're dead, you're dead. I don't even know if I want a funeral and a grave; that is, a place where those who love me can suffer.

One day in September 2021 I got a phone call from Pittsburgh: 'Freddie Fu has seven to ten days to live. Cancer.'

It was faster than that.

They called me back. 'He's dead.' That's life.

10. Passing
(*or About Friendship*)

Today I do a lot more passing than I used to.

When I was younger I was much more selfish. These days I think more about the team. As a young man, you see yourself as being at war with the world and you're tempted to dribble around the entire population of the planet. Then you start to understand that football is a collective game and you can be as good at it as you like but, playing with a team around you, you'll only get better and stronger.

The older I grew and the more I matured, the more I realized that I needed my teammates, that I relied on their support. Today, as far as I'm concerned, passing is more important than dribbling.

The passing I like best is when it develops out of a vision. Not the final pass – the easiest pass to understand, the direct assist that makes the crowd go *Wow!* No. What I do is foresee the development of a move that starts over here, on the right, and then, after a series of passes, creates a situation of danger over there, on the left, through a sort of domino effect. So my first pass sets off a plan into operation and, even if no one cheers for it, it's no less important than the last pass that will assist the actual scoring of the goal. In fact it's even more important, because that's where it all started. Without that first move – without the vision – the killer pass would never have come into being. That's the kind of passing I like.

There's an episode that I remember from when I played for Inter. Maicon Sisenando flicked a ball to me and I did a sort of bicycle kick to pass it to Dejan Stanković. Lots of people watching thought: 'What luck!'

No, it wasn't luck; it was control. I had total control of the situation and I chose that exact action, which so many thought must have been instinctive – improvised – to continue the move.

That's what I love: always having full control of attacking play, knowing the position of your teammates and opponents, so that you can decide on a pass to create an opening for a teammate, a bridgehead.

With a series of these passes under control, in one season at AC Milan I assisted Antonio Nocerino in scoring eleven goals, and he's not exactly a top goal-scorer.

Antonio was very intelligent. There are players who try to do everything on the pitch that they're capable of doing. But not Antonio. He never took possession of the ball for the final assist, to run the game or to dribble. He won balls and passed to his teammates, so that they could create chances and move into the opposing penalty area.

Going to join the scrum among the other defenders, after fighting so hard, was just one more sacrifice. Like doing overtime after your workday is finished. Not everyone is up for it.

For instance, Robinho certainly wasn't about to dump the ball for a sacrifice run. He was another kind of player; he wanted to stay in the game. If he was passing you the ball, he wanted it back right away to invent, create, show off. That's not true of Antonio Nocerino – he went into the penalty area and I knew I could find him there.

These days, like I said, I save my strength until I can go for the goal. Pioli hammers me to make sure I'm always up front and ready. But ten years ago I was a different kind of player, not desperate to shoot, like certain strikers who'll even shoot from the corner flag. I wanted to play football, I was circling around the penalty area, constantly in motion, making passes to Jérôme Boateng, Alexandre Pato, Robinho, Inzaghi . . .

Nocerino exploited this opportunity very well, displaying great intelligence. Eleven goals is a lot for a midfielder, especially in Italy.

If I'm asked to list the players who made the best passes, I'd have to start with Pavel Nedvěd, who was at the top of the heap, a Ballon d'Or winner, a generous person, both on the pitch and off. Never selfish, he always worked for the team's best interests, giving me advice, encouraging me and providing me with fabulous assists.

But David Trezeguet told me, 'Zlatan, you go out and collect the balls, and I'll wait for you in the penalty area.' Which of course really meant: 'You do the hard work and I'll score the goals.'

I was young and I agreed: 'Yes, sure, will do, David.'

The more footballs I controlled, the happier I was.

Trezeguet was only interested in goals. In fact he won the top-scorer ranking thanks to my assists and my constant movement. I worked hard for him.

The next year, though, I told him, 'Listen, David, I want to score goals too.' And I started running up goals for myself.

I also had an excellent rapport with Marco Verratti, who would deliver passes of the absolute highest quality. We arrived at Paris Saint-Germain the same year and were introduced to the press on the same day. I walk into a room with very few journalists and I see a complete stranger holding a press conference. He's little. 'Maybe he's not a footballer at all,' I think to myself, 'maybe he's a new executive, one of the sponsors, or something like that.'

'Who's that?' I ask.

'Marco Verratti,' they tell me.

'And where's he from?' I ask.

'From the Italian Serie B, from Pescara.'

It seems so strange. PSG usually picks up players like Thiago Silva and Ibrahimović, not Italians from Serie B. Go figure . . .

I do my press conference. The room, which had been empty, suddenly fills up and I introduce myself, say my hellos, make my promises, blah-blah-blah.

The little guy sits and listens.

Then the first training session starts, with Ancelotti, Pastore, Lavezzi and all the rest. And among them this new guy, Verratti, who's come to us straight from Serie B.

As soon as he controls a couple of balls, I freeze. I'm

not tempted to say, 'Let's have a look. Let's wait and see. Maybe this was just dumb chance. Beginner's luck.' No, it's clear. Definitive verdict: this young man has something special. Anyone who plays football can see certain things straight away. If a new player arrives at Milan, I'll immediately figure out what he's made of.

Verratti is the only player I know who always calls for the ball, even if he's marked, out of position, off-balance, injured . . . He always wants the ball. He's not afraid of anything. And nine times out of ten, he emerges with the ball at his feet, even in pressure situations. There aren't many players on Earth who can do that.

Still, Ancelotti always said one thing to me: 'Zlatan, he'll listen to you. Why don't you convince Verratti to stop making those soft passes he likes so much.' So I asked Marco to send me sharper, crisper passes.

I'm really happy that he won the Euros because he's a great, humble kid who's always won everybody's hearts. When he arrived in Paris he still wasn't ready for top-flight football. I'm not talking about technical issues. I'm talking about handling a serious contract, dealing with bureaucracy and everything else that goes along with being in a top club. I helped him by lending him the consultants I have on my staff: banking experts, financial advisors, legal minds. That way he could just concentrate on the football.

I'm also happy for him because I know how much he suffered in the months leading up to the Euros and how afraid he was of missing them, the way I did. We had the same physio. The guy told me that Marco would be able to be back for the second or third match, if things went well.

After the triumph in London, I saw Verratti at his wedding. He invited only a few friends. 'You absolutely have to be there,' he commanded.

It was a wonderful ceremony, with Lavezzi, Pastore, Sirigu and all the rest. We've preserved the chemistry that bound us together when we played on the same team. The once-little Verratti from Serie B – the unknown player I'd taken for an executive in an empty room – has pulled it off: there he is, happily married and a European champion!

But I had my best chemistry, and the finest understanding – because it was natural, instinctive and unforced – with Pogba at Manchester United. We hit it off immediately, without knowing each other, without sizing each other up. It was a delight and it was never dull to play with Pogba, to be the recipient of his brilliant passes.

At Inter, instead of having one particular player who fed me passes, I had a whole crew who shared the task: Cristian Chivu, Maxwell, Stanković and of course Maicon, who was an awe-inspiring passing machine. He could always find me.

The best passer of the ball today is Kevin De Bruyne. He sees things that the others don't. This Belgian player has the kind of vision that I try to have when I play. The goal he came up with against Denmark at the Euros explains everything. He plunged into the penalty area, received the ball and everyone expected him to kick it into the net, but instead he – and he alone – spotted Thorgan

Hazard arriving and passed to him: goal! De Bruyne sees what's about to happen a split second before anybody else.

If dribbling is a bolt for freedom, passing bonds you to your teammates; it is like a rope team on a mountain. Dribbling offers you solitude, whereas passing creates friendship on the pitch.

In life, however, true friendship is a pretty rare thing, I believe. I have only a few friends. I mean the kind of friends you have for a lifetime, that you talk to every day and whom you can trust implicitly, blindfolded. Mino is a friend, a father, an agent – everything. Mino is the whole package; he's something else. But I only have a couple of close, true friends, in the classical sense of the word.

The friends I had when I was a boy? I've had to ditch them all, because the more successful I got, the more jealousy became an issue. I couldn't understand it. We'd all grown up together, we'd always been a team, we'd all gone together to the resort town of Ayia Napa, on the island of Cyprus, to have fun on the beach and at the clubs. But the more famous I became, the more I heard them talking about me behind my back. I kept hearing mean things that they wouldn't say to my face. I couldn't believe it. In the end I made up my mind: these former friends of mine were nothing but a source of negative energy, and I didn't need them. And I cut them out of my life.

All they seemed to want was help with money, and they started spreading rumours that I wouldn't help anyone. But friendship has nothing to do with money. You can still be my friend, even if you don't have money. I wasn't rich yet; I was just starting to earn and I was careful with my money, because easy come, easy go – it's as fast to lose it as it is to earn it. I knew what it's like not to have money, to look into an empty fridge.

So I turned my back on them all, except for Guðmundur Mete, an Icelander who used to play with me on the first team at Malmö. He was never jealous, and every so often we still talk.

It's hard to have real, loyal friends without any ulterior motives. That's why I say that my best friends are my lawyers: I pay them, they work for me and, when I need them, they're always there to help me.

These days, my life is pretty isolated, and I don't let a lot of people in. If I let them in, it means they've earned my trust and affection. There are a few people I trust, but I don't have a true best friend now. Since I had the bitter disappointment of losing my longtime friends I've turned inwards, to my family, and I've led a very secluded, protected life.

Maxwell is my best footballing friend, the one I trust most, but we don't speak on a daily basis. And I talk now and then with Ignazio Abate, Mete and a few others. Can you be friends with your coach? I say you can. Once I called up Ancelotti, who was no longer at PSG. 'Ciao, Coach. How are you?'

He replied, 'Don't call me Coach, I'm not a coach any more. Either call me Carlo or else call me Friend.'

Carlo is a coach unlike any other, and he had a special relationship with the team. One night I was out having dinner in Paris with six or seven players. We called him up to say hello and, twenty minutes later, he was sitting at the table with us, drinking a beer.

I have a great relationship with Pioli, too. Last summer we ran into each other on the island of Formentera. We were both holidaying there at the same time. Before leaving for Formentera, when I found out that he'd be there too, I kidded around with him. 'Coach, that's a place for rich people. You won't fit in . . .'

I'd call him from my boat, he'd send me his location on his smartphone and he was always on the far side of the island. It was like playing hide-and-seek. We never once got together the whole holiday.

Every so often, when, say, I might be dressing down Saelemaekers for failing to pass me the ball once in the match, Pioli would call me out: 'Cool it, Zlatan. I'm pretty sure I can rev up the team from the bench.' At other times he'd tell me, 'Zlatan, you go ahead and juice up the guys out on the pitch, and I'll just sit here, nice and relaxed, in the dugout.'

Actually Pioli never sits back nice and relaxed anywhere; he's always 100 per cent engaged in the match. He's a madman.

Once, in a match against Roma, at the end of the first half, I feel something wrong with my adductor muscles. I let him know. During half-time we talk it over and get the doctors' input on whether I should sit out the second half. The coach decides, 'Zlatan, now go back in and stay put in front of the goal, okay? Don't force things.'

During the first move of the second half, though, he starts yelling at me, 'Zlatan, get moving. Run! Attack!'

Wait: aren't I the one who is supposed to stay put?

Of all the dressing rooms I've ever spent time in, the one where friendship was most unmistakably in the air was at PSG. We often went out to dinner together, sometimes at Lavezzi's house, where we gorged on Argentine grilled meat. It was more or less the same group that attended Verratti's wedding. It felt then as if we'd last seen each other just ten minutes ago, not ten years previously.

In this current Milan team there's also an incredible atmosphere, but it's different, because I'm more of a leader, a symbol, an example. I don't go out for dinner with the team because I know they respect me too much. It wouldn't be a comfortable situation for them – they'd be intimidated, uneasy.

I'm convinced of one thing: if I'd remained the Ibrahimović I once was, then this young Milan team, with so few players who have international experience, wouldn't have won anything, because I would have crushed them with my sheer aggression. But as I've aged, I've matured. I realize that from my reactions.

These days I'm tough, but also gentle. I have an equilibrium that's new to me. Balance . . . I no longer treat my teammates the way I used to. I know that there are some who need to be stimulated and encouraged, possibly in private, while there are others who need to be dressed down in front of the group. So I'm tough and gentle.

I didn't come to Milan to score forty goals and lose matches. I'm here to help the team grow, as a collective and as individuals. To win, all together. That's my challenge: this is my new role.

Ten years ago, in my previous life at Milan, I served a very different function: I was supposed to be the ball-buster who squeezed every last drop out of a generation of champions that had won everything.

In the Italian national team under Roberto Mancini I glimpsed the same spirit as in my Milan: few superstars, but an excellent group. Their secret, and our secret, is the atmosphere, the magical chemistry that exists, fusing together the young and not-so-young into a single entity. The Blues – the Azzurri – sang aboard their bus, the same as we always did, and used the music of our notoriously catchy tune: 'Pioli Is On Fire'.

Mancini has done an outstanding job. Roberto has made such huge changes. At Inter he had no relationship with the players. Zero. Mihajlović did everything. Mancini merely supervised training, oversaw the tactical part, and that was it. Zero dialogue with the team. Siniša took care of that. Now Mancini seems like another person, a different man. He talks to everyone, gets along with everyone, even outside the national team. He has a different approach, and he gives you a sense of feeling, where he used to be cold and detached. He won by exploiting the players he had to the best of their ability.

At Italy's first Euro 2020 match I said it right away. 'These guys are going all the way.' The more they won, the better their group chemistry and enthusiasm, exactly as it had been for us. And when you gain confidence, you also build up the courage to play a new, more attacking kind of football, as Mancini and Pioli were pushing for.

The first three matches in Rome, with fans, were

decisive, after a year of empty stadiums. At Milan we played, we won and then we said, 'Okay, now let's go home and eat dinner.' It was a grim routine.

But the Azzurri had fans singing in the stadiums, celebrating, feeding energy back to them, transmitting a constant surge of adrenaline, hauling them along with their excitement. So they got bigger and better, from match to match.

The thing that thrilled me most was the Azzurri's defence.

I like Leonardo Bonucci and Giorgio Chiellini because I've played against them and I know exactly how good they are. They're a perfect pair, complementing each other wonderfully: Chiellini can kill you in a one-on-one, whereas Bonucci really plays football. An exceptional mix in a playing system, with a great, overarching equilibrium: Italy is always on the attack, but it also knows how to defend.

Did you see Chiellini with poor Bukayo Saka in the Euros final at Wembley? That's just how Chiellini is: even if you get past him, even if you dribble around him, you know it's not over, because he'll do whatever he can to stop you. What can you do if he gets you by the neck? Nothing. You get mad, but you keep going. That's Chiellini: the man is a monster.

I really love battling against a defender like him, the same as I used to love facing off against Maldini, Nesta, Cannavaro, Thuram and Jakob Stam. Adrenaline, in its purest state. You know you're always going to have to give an extra something when you're up against these giants, because they'll never give up. But if you actually manage to get past them – maybe not at the first attempt, but at the second – it makes you feel great. You heave a sigh of contentment: 'Oh, that's nice . . .'

And, of course, I liked Donnarumma, who's matured immensely. I always asked: 'How much is Donnarumma worth?' A goalie like him is priceless. You pay him what he asks and then you thank him for not having asked for more, because he's only going to get better. Today he's no longer the goalie he was before the Euros; now he could demand twice as much without a problem. If he asks you for ten million euros, give that to him. Those ten million euros aren't an expense, they're an investment.

Plus, Gigio had an added value that goes beyond his sheer athletic skill: he grew up at Milan, and he could have become the new Maldini, a flag, a team captain. It's not true that he would have left the club in any case. Gigio would have stayed, he told me so: 'If they give me what I'm asking, I'll stay. I love it here.'

You can't replace a goalie like him. Donnarumma would bring you a fifteen-year future, not two or three years.

In all the teams I've played for, I've never worried that much about the goalie, because if the strongest player on the team is the one wearing the number one, it means you'll never win a thing. But with Donnarumma things were different: he'd saved Milan so many times, and he'd helped the team to grow gradually. You can only thank him for what he's given us. He was our strength and our confidence. We knew that, even if we didn't make it, he'd always be there behind us to make things good.

The only other one who ever thrilled me like that was Gianluigi Buffon. In training, Capello put me against Thuram and Cannavaro. One against two. When I passed those two – *if* I passed them – then I'd find myself face-to-face with Buffon: a wall, who'd catch all the shots. Donnarumma gave me the same feeling.

Gigio isn't yet at the level of Buffon at his finest, but he has enormous potential. You can see that he has something very special inside him. And he's grown greatly in terms of personality as well. At first he was touchy, suspicious, always on the defensive, especially if anyone criticized him. He behaved like a diva, even if he wasn't anything special yet. Then I arrived – someone who had won something – and he changed.

He started reacting like a leader. He accepted my criticisms, and he might even occasionally give a retort that spoke of a new level of confidence: 'Okay, but you have to do this too, you know.'

And so, sharing advice, putting our heads together, the group grew. Because when I arrived at Milan I put pressure on everyone without letting anyone push back, even players like Donnarumma and Romagnoli, who could boast a certain status.

When he arrived in Paris, Donnarumma spent too much time on the bench. Mino came to ask me, 'In your opinion, should Gigio declare open warfare against PSG?'

'Of course he should declare open warfare,' I replied. 'He needs to go to Mauricio Pochettino every single match and ask him: "Why aren't you playing me?"'

I have to put Donnarumma in an uncomfortable

position: him and all the others. Otherwise life is too easy for them. If Gigio accepts the bench, it means he agrees that he's inferior, and he isn't. So he might as well remain a team player at Milan and accept the contract they offered him.

It wasn't a case of showing off your technical qualities. After two training sessions, everyone understood that Donnarumma was the best player. He needed to assert himself, even though in the dressing room it was probably natural that the South Americans were all on Keylor Navas's side.

Gigio was honoured as the finest player in the Euros in a team that was on the attack, not a team that was falling back on defence. And it was only right. He was the real star of the final. On penalties, in the final, he was a beast.

Gareth Southgate made all the wrong decisions, that's true, but it wasn't easy in that packed Wembley stadium, with all of England on his back and fifty-five years of history without a title to show for it. And it wasn't easy to manage the penalties that would decide the title. You might easily have practised taking a thousand penalties and scored every one of them, but when you get out onto the actual pitch in real play, during a crucial match, you're on another planet.

Last season I found that out, at my own expense. I've always taken penalties with an excellent success rate. But at the beginning of the season I started making mistakes and something happened in my head. I couldn't really figure out what – something just went.

When I walked to the penalty spot I felt confident, full

of certainty. I started out nice and relaxed, but then, at the exact moment my foot hit the ball, I felt as if I was losing all my strength. Everything was perfect until impact with the ball, then either I lost my strength or I became insecure and changed my mind at the last second. Nothing like that had ever happened before.

I tried to keep going anyway: 'The next one will go better, my head will clear, I'll get over this strange case of penalty block.' But it didn't improve. So I told Kessié, 'You take it, Franck.' I wanted to shake off a little of the pressure, catch my breath before trying again.

I scored a penalty against Cagliari in January 2021, but it was a shitty attempt, weak and feeble. I was lucky the goalie dived the wrong way. 'Fuck, I still can't pull off the final touch,' I thought. And I get it wrong against Bologna. Again . . .

After the fifth failed penalty, I make up my mind. That's it, no more penalties until I regain my confidence and feel free. After all, I'll always have Kessié, who takes great penalties.

It doesn't matter who puts the ball in – what matters is that the team scores. Franck missed against Juve, but I told him, 'Don't worry, just keep going. I don't have anything to prove to the world. I'm only here to help the team grow.' At this point I have no idea when I'll get back to the penalty spot.

A different mindset is going to have to click in my head. At this point a penalty is no longer a challenge against the goalie, but against myself. It's a hurdle that I need to get past, and it can only happen in a real match.

Practice doesn't help. When I'd get one wrong, I'd say to Donnarumma, 'Gigio, come on, let's go take some penalties.' I'd put every one of them in the back of the net with my customary precision, every time. It's in real matches that I'm not clicking. The problem is all in my head. After Gigio leaves, I'm worried that Kessié might go, too. It's the obvious thing: if you win, you can ask for new deals.

If I was asked to choose a friend from history to have dinner with, I'd definitely pick Muhammad Ali, because he was the same person, inside and out. He practised what he preached, even if it meant going to prison, in a time of social division – a time of war and racial tensions. When you manage to send out important messages from the platform afforded to a world champion athlete, messages that reach around the world, then you're something far more than simply an athlete. You're an icon, a symbol – everything. I would have loved to spend some time chatting with him.

If, on the other hand, you asked me to choose someone alive now to take on a round-the-world tour aboard my boat, I'd bring Mino. He's knowledgeable about everything to do with the seas and oceans, fishing, barrier reefs, and he is knowledgeable about everything else there is to know. Somebody brings up the name of a small Hungarian town? Mino can give you all kinds of information about it, and he might even be able to suggest a nice restaurant.

But my real best friend – more of a friend than all the other friends – is named Red. He's my dog, an English bulldog. If I want affection, he'll never let me down.

I've always wanted an English bulldog. We ordered a

puppy from a breeder in Wales. We went to see the puppy a couple of times, and it was on one of those trips that we met Red and he stole my heart. It was a bolt out of the blue. I saw him and he was exactly as I'd imagined him: strong, massive, with an enormous head, even though he was only two years old. He was the perfect dog.

The only obstacle was that he wasn't for sale, because he had a problem. He'd been traumatized, maybe by fireworks at New Year. Something had snapped in his brain, and since then he hadn't been the same. No more dog shows for him. A wonderful dog, but anxious, scared and stressed. We asked if we could buy him, but the answer was no.

Some time after we picked up the puppy we'd ordered, the breeders came to see us in Manchester and they brought Red with them. They offered to let us keep him on a trial basis for a while, to see how things turned out.

So for nearly two weeks Red stays, motionless, in a corner of the kitchen. He only goes out into the garden to poop or pee and then hurries back into the house. We realize that he needs professional help, so we hire a dog trainer to work with him. Just for one day. If he makes some progress, we'll keep him; otherwise, we'll take him back to Wales.

Unbelievably, in half a day, the dog changes completely. In the end we take back the puppy and we keep Red. During the day Red does nothing at all. He merely sleeps, eats and goes for short walks in the park. Today he's a fully fledged member of our family. I miss him so badly that I have a kind of statue of him in Milan.

And so the list has grown: Red has entered the group

of my best friends. He is the kindest and bravest Englishman – or Englishdog – I've ever met.

After turning thirty in 2011 I decided to stop celebrating my birthday, because that day, 3 October, had become a sort of reminder on the calendar: 'Don't forget that you're old.' For football, anyway.

I've always treated my birthday just like an ordinary day. I'd spend it quietly at home with my family, without surprise parties or anything like that. And I intended to stick to the same script for my fortieth: a nice round number, and a boundary that few footballers have passed while still remaining active players.

The day before, one of my closest friends, Patrizio, tells me, 'Tomorrow you need to be ready at eight p.m.'

'Okay,' I think to myself, 'we'll be going out to dinner with our families.' I'm free on my birthday. I take Maximilian, Vincent and a friend of theirs to Milanello because they want to play. I don't have any obligations, so I'm in no hurry and I do everything in the most relaxed way imaginable.

We go home and Helena tells me, 'Start getting ready, because we'll need to go soon.'

'All right, what should I wear?'

'Put on something nice, it's your birthday.'

Something nice? Okay: jeans and a white shirt would be nice. But then I start to sense something's a little off, because Helena dresses not *nice*, but truly fancy – let's even say elegant – as if she was planning to go on the catwalk at a fashion show.

I warn her immediately, 'Listen, let's not have any surprises or special effects, because you know how much I hate them.'

'Don't worry, it won't be anyone besides your brother and a few friends who are here from Sweden. We'll just have dinner, and that's all.'

Oh, all right then.

They take me to the Hyatt Centric hotel. Mino is already there, and he's given me a spectacular gift: a hunting rifle, or actually the Rolls-Royce of hunting rifles. It's a wonderful thing.

There's my brother and his wife; my friends Thomas, Daniel Majstorović (who was on the Swedish national team with me) and Andreas; Max Martin, my first physio at the Malmö club; Patrizio and his wife. We have dinner and then we're waiting for the birthday cake.

They ask me, 'Would you mind going to the kitchen to say hello to the cooks? You know, they came here specially all the way from Rome.'

All right, happy to do so; the dinner was really outstanding.

Then they lead me to a lift that takes me up to the top floor, to the terrace. My entourage precedes me. I walk out and I recognize Nada Topčagić, the Serbo-Bosnian singer, and the music of '*Jutro je*' starts up, a song I love. She begins to sing.

One after another, I find myself looking at well-known faces. Everyone's there, and I mean everyone.

'Ciao . . .' Gianluca Zambrotta.

'Ciao . . .' Olivier Dacourt.

'Ciao . . .' Rino Gattuso.

I'm stunned. It seems unreal. I walk forward across the terrace like a zombie.

Ambrosini, Oddo, Abate, Cassano, Verratti, Donnarumma, Sirigu, Kulusevski, Pogba – faces I haven't seen in years and years. Moggi, Galliani . . .

The song ends, I take the microphone and, even though I'm confused and deeply touched, I try to string together a few words: 'Let me thank every last one of you. I didn't expect this at all. It really was a wonderful surprise. I can see a lot of guys are here that I didn't really treat that well. I didn't think you'd come. And I swear to you, I didn't pay any of you to be here. Maybe this means that I really do have a heart and that I must have done something good, after all.'

Applause, cheers, hugs.

Then come the coaches – Pioli, Maldini – and my teammates who've just played against Bergamo and won an important match. I've returned to AC Milan because of a 5–0 loss against Atalanta, to help the team get back on its feet; and tonight, on that same pitch, my Milan has dominated the opposition and given quite a show. Goals were scored by Davide Calabria, Tonali and Leão, three young men who have matured enormously in the past few months.

All of them here on my birthday. Could I ever have received a finer birthday present from my teammates?

In the first season, Tonali was trapped in a dream. He looked around and kept telling himself, 'This is the team I've dreamed of since I was a child.'

In 2021 he emerged from his dream and entered real life. Now he tells himself, 'I'm a Milan player', and in fact he shows it in every match. He barrels through like a panzer tank. Sandro will soon become a fully fledged national team player. It's only a matter of time. Likewise Calabria's arrived, having attained the peak of his maturity. Tonali, on the other hand, has some serious improvement still to do.

I can claim no credit for Leão. I've already explained it: he's the only one I never found a key to communicate with. I gave up; if he doesn't make an effort, I can't do a thing. If he doesn't decide to change and grow, then I can't help him. Finally, though, he did it. He made up his mind to help himself and now he's a very different player. He sidesteps and leaps over everyone with an embarrassing ease – it almost seems as if he's playing against the under-nineteen Primavera youth team. From the first day of preparation, he's got his head in the game with the right mindset. He's trained hard and the results have come. Now he's doing great, absolutely great, and he needs to continue in that direction.

And for Pioli that's quite a problem, because I think never in his life has he had so many first-rate players all together on the same team.

One day in Milanello we were having a tactical practice match with a full team. I was on the reserve team, watching the other formation – the one that would later demolish Lazio – and I thought to myself: 'Wait, we can beat them. A hundred per cent.' Pioli's good luck is that he has an extra gear at his disposal.

My teammates have grown up, they're top of the championship, they're playing in the Champions League and they've crushed Atalanta.

During the party Galliani insisted on watching the Bergamo match at all costs, and so he had a screen brought out onto the terrace.

I'm truly happy. Even if I don't usually care for this kind of thing, I have to admit that Helena threw me a fantastic surprise birthday party. She worked on it for a month. Berlusconi was supposed to come, too, but on the morning of the party he called to say he wouldn't be able to make it.

It was a real pleasure to see Luciano Moggi again, after all the years I hadn't seen him. He was the one who first brought me to Italy; he opened the door for me. At that point all I had to do was walk through it and be Ibra.

It was also great to see Adriano Galliani, with whom I've always been on excellent terms, except for that time he dumped me in Paris.

Listening to them talk to each other was a thrill.

Galliani was saying, 'I remember once, Zlatan, you were supposed to play against us, but you were banned, and Luciano did everything in his power to get the red card rescinded. I found out, and I didn't sit around twiddling my thumbs . . .'

And Moggi: 'Do you remember, Adriano, that fantastic goal that Trezeguet scored at the San Siro from Alessandro Del Piero's bicycle kick?'

Galliani: 'What I really remember is Sheva's penalty against Manchester United.'

And then there was Antonio Cassano, saying whatever came into his head, completely unfiltered, which is just his way.

It was a truly magical atmosphere. I was happy and I was deeply moved. That surprise party on the terrace was the finest birthday present I could have hoped for. And in that happiness, the finest thing of all was the sight of the pride and joy on my sons' faces.

For years they've asked me, 'Papa, what was Gattuso like? What were Maldini, Zambrotta and Ambrosini like?' They'd send me YouTube videos and pepper me with questions. Now they were seeing so many of those thoroughbreds, in flesh and blood, all together on the terrace.

'Take advantage of their presence,' I told Maximilian and Vincent. 'Go and talk to them all – in Italian, in English, in French – and you'll see, they'll understand you. Ask them anything you want.'

It was wonderful to see them so deeply excited, eyes wide, as they moved from Gattuso to Pogba. It was also a way for them to learn more about my own story, because now I have fine teammates, but my sons know that there was a time when their papa played with the world's best footballers.

The cake was enormous, with my football boots on top. We stayed there and talked and joked around until four in the morning. I really had a great time.

I was scared when I entered the Hyatt Centric hotel. That gigantic number forty, created by the illuminated windows, had made me sweat: what awaits me in there? But I was happy when I left, just before dawn, thinking about one thing: if I'd thrown the party, everyone would have come, even if they hadn't wanted to. They'd have thought: 'If Zlatan calls us, we have to go.'

But I didn't know who had been invited and who hadn't. So everyone who was out there on the terrace could have dreamed up an excuse, and I'd never have known. It meant that they came purely because they wanted to spend time with me and celebrate my birthday.

When I said that I have few friends, except for my lawyers, I might have exaggerated.

Extra Time
(or About the Future)

Milan, Wednesday 3 November 2021

Yesterday it rained and rained, all day long. This morning, though, the sky is clear and blue. You can see the mountains on the horizon, already white with snow.

I love to look out on Milan from my terrace: the children playing in the park down below, the Duomo on the left, the towers of the San Siro Stadium poking up in the distance . . . I have the feeling that I have the whole city under my thumb. That, pretty as it is, it's even prettier from up here.

I feel like stretching out my arms, as I do after scoring a goal. I breathe in the cool air and shut my eyes for a moment.

Helena claims that my apartment is basically a hotel room. She doesn't like it because it's furnished for *me*, with too many sports souvenirs and memorabilia, a big TV, a dining table crowded with computers and games, to the point that we sometimes have to sit on stools in the kitchen to eat.

But I love the place. I like living there and it makes me feel safe. It's perfect for what I need. I'm playing at Milan for just one reason, and I'm completely focused on my mission. The long wait of the pandemic is over. At last the stadium will fill up with a crowd wrapped in flags and streamers, shouting frantically, and I'll be pumped up with the adrenaline I've been waiting for, which I've been missing for so long. Adrenaline is my engine, my motivation for continuing to do what I love most. Money is no longer my driving force; no, it's the deafening shouts, the screams, the songs and the cheers from the stands. That's what makes me feel that football is a matter of life or death.

A game I'll love for ever.

Next Sunday will be the derby. It's always a special match, because it determines who rules the city. We're ready.

Two days ago we played an important match against Roma, a home game for them, in a magnificent atmosphere: the Stadio Olimpico was practically full, with 50,000 spectators. I'd really been missing the fans, even if they were opposing fans and would boo and hiss and whistle, scream insults and abuse.

During the warm-up I was already feeling pretty good. Like I explained: I'm the one who decides whether a match is going to go well or badly. In my head. And I'd already decided that things were going to go well for us in Rome. Before leaving the dressing room, I told Daniele Bonera, Pioli's assistant coach, 'I'm going to go out there and smash it all up.'

In the pre-match interview, they asked me about the 50,000 spectators. I said, 'Let's hope they whistle and boo me, because the louder they whistle, the more it revs me up, and the more alive it makes me feel.'

We gather in a circle, arms around each other's shoulders, in the centre circle, just moments before kick-off.

I order the team, 'We're going to attack from the very first second.'

And in fact as soon as the referee blows his whistle, we go for the ball, in a herd, making it clear to Roma that we want it – that it's ours. We create chances, then they give us a free kick.

Ismaël Bennacer steps up to me. 'Yesterday, in training, I didn't miss one. Let me give it a try, Zlatan.'

I reply, 'Okay, you take the free kicks in training, and I'll take them during the match.'

Ismaël smiles and walks away.

I'm certain that the goalie is expecting a screamer, arcing in over the wall, because I'm off to one side of the goal. So I decide to surprise him with a powerful, skimming ground shot, from the opposite side. In fact he takes a step towards the wall and, when he realizes that the ball is travelling in a different direction, he tries to move to meet it, but loses his balance and slams to the ground.

I celebrate our lead with my teammates by lifting two fingers to the centre of my forehead. Then all the opposing fans in the stands start shouting out 'Gypsy' at me.

I lift my hands to my ears: 'I can't hear you.' I call to them to raise their voices: 'Louder! I can't hear you ... Louder!'

A roar of voices and shrill whistles of derision explode.

'Louder! I can't hear you ...'

It fills me with adrenaline. I throw both arms wide, smiling broadly. I feel fully alive, I feel powerful.

The referee gives me a yellow card. Then and there, I don't say a word to him because I'm still under the effects of the adrenaline. During half-time, though, my adrenaline has subsided.

I go over to him and I complain, 'Listen, although you gave *me* a yellow card, when fifty thousand spectators called me a "Gypsy", you didn't do a thing. You only punished me. What do you say about that?'

I hadn't provoked anyone, I hadn't given anyone the finger, I hadn't grabbed my crotch. I'd simply thrown both arms wide in front of a stand packed with opposition fans insulting me.

I warn the referee, 'Watch out, don't play with fire, because I'm not like the other players. Behave properly and do the right thing.' He couldn't card me just to satisfy those who were whistling and booing me, and those who were shouting from the bench. Then, in the tunnel, he answers me. 'Be careful or I'll throw you out of here.'

Ten years ago, in the face of that threat, no one could have held me back. I'd have gone wild. But this time I say nothing, I control myself. I can feel the responsibility I have towards my teammates, and I'm not looking to create problems for the team.

Adrenaline and balance.

Pioli warns me, 'Zlatan, I'm going to leave you on the pitch only for another ten or fifteen minutes because I don't trust this referee.'

'Don't worry, Coach. I'll only tackle for the ball, and I'll only do it if I'm sure I'm not going to start a brawl.' I wasn't going to give the referee an excuse to show me a second yellow card.

And in fact when I go back onto the pitch for the second half, I steer clear of the duels and brawls over the ball.

They disallow an offside goal that I score; they disallow another goal that Rafael Leão scores with my assist; and I was awarded the penalty that Kessié converted for the 2–0 score. It's a clear penalty, because the defender, after hip-slamming me, knees me too, blocking my leg so that I fall forward.

When the referee goes to check it out on the VAR monitor, I'm absolutely certain: 'He's going to deny us the penalty. He won't give one for a foul against me.'

Instead, to our surprise, he does give it.

I'm still on the ground when Kessié walks over and tells me, 'It's yours.'

Ten years ago I would have taken that ball and kicked it. My ego would have demanded that I score the second goal and then leave the pitch.

But what I want now is to see the team gain confidence and feel that it's them in charge. I've already scored a goal, I've been awarded a penalty, and I've played against 50,000 enemy fans screaming insults. I've been in the spotlight plenty. Now it's their turn, because I'm going to leave the pitch soon and they need to feel strong enough to bring home three points.

I reply, 'No, Franck. You take it.'

Kessié scores, I'm substituted, Theo gets sent off and the suffering begins. Roma attacks more and more aggressively, Mourinho protests continuously, lighting the fires in the hearts of the fans in the Stadio Olimpico. So, ten minutes from the end, I order my teammates on the bench, 'Let's all stand up and cheer this team on. They need us!'

Standing at the edge of the pitch, we wave our arms and shout our heads off, revving up the guys on the field who are bringing home a very important victory.

Mourinho, furious, congratulates me and says a very quick hello. Before the match I was too focused to talk to him, partly because I know he's a master practitioner of mind-games and I didn't want to let him get to me. But then I'm not bad at mind-games myself.

The whole challenge with the Roma fans was a mind-game: they kept shouting 'Gypsy' at me, and I'd throw my arms wide and smile.

Now, back on the terrace of my house, I ponder the matter: we took the knee for two years to show our solidarity with people of colour who were being discriminated against. Good, we did the right thing. I like it. But what are we doing for other minorities?

I've said it before, I don't like politics in sport. I'm just asking a few questions: how is shouting 'Gypsy' a less serious offence? Is it a less discriminatory insult? What should we do? If they had shouted any other racist insult, the referee would surely have stopped play. Instead *they* shouted 'Gypsy' at me and the referee yellow-carded *me*.

What good does it do to take the knee, wear a logo that

reads 'Respect', pose attractively for a 'No racism' spot, if nothing ever changes in the stadiums?

I've won lots of Scudetti, but this one would have been the most gratifying, because no other team has changed so much since my arrival.

The match against Roma was the final confirmation: every player walked out onto the pitch convinced he was a thoroughbred. That's the kind of confidence we should always play with. The young players are afraid of nothing and they attack because they know we're strong; they know that together, as a team, we're much better than any of our individual qualities.

I can't say whether, with me on the pitch, they feel safer, but for sure if we were to win the Scudetto, it would be the most fantastic win ever. Perhaps winning the Scudetto with this Milan would be the ideal culmination of my career. But I'm still afraid of quitting and I still feel too powerful to retire.

The football boots with the words 'Zlatan 40' embroidered on them, which I was given for my birthday, contain the message: 'I'm forty years old and I'm still here.'

I want to play at the next World Cup.

I have an excellent relationship with the manager of the Swedish national team. Before every meeting he calls me, enquires how things are and always asks the same question: 'Do you want to continue?'

The last time I answered: 'Yes, I do. Don't worry. Don't ask me again. When I no longer feel able to play for the national team, I'll let you know.' For now I think I can help young players to improve, the way I did for Milan. I have nothing to prove, nothing to impose. I just want to inspire.

The advice that van Basten gave me at the beginning of my career is advice that I've already given to other, younger players. History repeats itself.

The future seems distant and still, like those snow-capped mountains down there, beyond the roofs of Milan. But actually it's coming towards me. It scares me a little. But I look it right in the eye.

And I throw both arms wide.

Index

ZI indicates Zlatan Ibrahimović.

Abate, Ignazio 215, 228
Acerbi, Francesco 171–2
AC Milan
  Academy 96–7
  Allegri and 79–81, 82, 143
  Atalanta 5–0 AC Milan
    (2019) 19, 20–21
  Atalanta 0–2 AC Milan (2021)
    18–19, 228, 230
  Berlusconi and 88–9, 110,
    181, 186, 230
  Boban leaves 13
  Çalhanoğlu leaves for
    Inter 46
  Champions League (2012) vs
    Arsenal 80
  Champions League (2021–22),
    qualification for 17, 18–19,
    20–21, 228, 230
  Champions League (2021–22)
    200–201
  Covid-19 and 54, 219
  derbies/ZI's personal
    rivalries at 67–76, 234
  Donnarumma and 16–17,
    220–22
  expenses at 118

friendship at 209, 212–13,
  217–18
Gattuso and 79
Gazidis and 14–15, 206
passing at 209, 212–13
penalties at 222–4, 237–8
Pioli and *see* Pioli, Stefano
referees and 168–9, 171–2
Sacchi and 29–30
Scudetto, wins (2010–11)
  80–81, 153–4
team spirit/mindset 11–19,
  46–7, 95, 177–8, 185, 221,
  228–30
ultras 16–17
van Basten and 29
ZI departs for PSG (2012)
  106–10, 111
ZI joins (2010) 69, 88–9, 206
ZI renews contract (2020)
  59–61, 95, 103, 104, 199
ZI returns to (2019) 10–19,
  53, 69, 206, 228–30
ZI's goals for 29, 153–4, 156,
  158–9
ZI's injuries and 196–7,
  200–201

AC Milan – *cont'd*
  ZI's signing for Inter (2006)
    and 186
adrenaline
  AC Milan and 8, 9, 10, 19, 96,
    206
  age and 4–5
  balance and 5
  business and 132
  cars and 53, 128, 129
  commentators and 140
  fans and 69, 70, 234, 235–6
  goals and 25, 31, 147, 148,
    149, 152, 154
  hunting and 133
  injuries and 188, 195
  Manchester United and 116, 121
  opponents and 219
  PSG and 108
  retirement and 49, 51–2, 96,
    104, 166
  sex and 87
Adriaanse, Jacobus 'Co' 150,
  151
Aftonbladet 134, 135–6
Agricola, Dr Riccardo 184–5
Ajax, AFC 162, 184
  van Basten and 29
  ZI joins 46, 87, 128, 150, 151
  ZI leaves 59, 81
  ZI's dribbling at 41
  ZI's goals for 25–6, 30, 31,
    151–3
  ZI's media relationship at
    134, 137

  ZI's shirts from 84
Ali, Muhammad 224
Allegri, Massimiliano 79–81, 82,
  143
'Amadeus' (Italian TV
  presenter) 57–8, 61, 62,
  64
Ambrosini, Massimo 11, 228,
  231
America. *See* Major League
  Soccer (MLS)
Ancelotti, Carlo 9, 10, 81, 211,
  212, 215–16
Anderlecht 119, 187–8
Andersson, Kennet 149, 150
Arsenal 80, 153
Atalanta 18–19, 20–21, 228,
  230

Bakayoko, Tiémoué 200
Ballack, Michael 66
Ballon d'Or 210
Barcelona, FC 29, 43, 44, 69, 79,
  103, 107, 153, 187
Barella, Nicolò 75
Bayern Munich 66, 77–8
Beenhakker, Leo 150, 151
beIN Sports 140–41
Belgium (national football team)
  213–14
Benfica 152–4
Bennacer, Ismaël 235
Berlusconi, Silvio 88–9, 110,
  181, 186, 230
Bethard (betting company) 63, 76

bicycle kicks v, 19–23, 24, 25, 29,
31, 40, 84, 98, 149, 209, 230
Blanc, Laurent 203
Boateng, Jérôme 210
Boban, Zvonimir 11, 13
Bologna FC 65, 203–6, 223
Bonera, Daniele 234
Bonucci, Leonardo 219
Bordeaux 37, 142, 174
Borg, Björn 138–9
Boškov, Vujadin 87
Braida, Ariedo 186
Brazil (national football team)
150
Breda, NAC 25–6
Buffon, Gianluigi 39, 221
Burdisso, Nicolás 77

Cafu 11
Cagliari Calcio 223
Cahill, Gary 20, 21
Calabria, Davide 228, 229
Calciopoli match-fixing scandal
180–82, 185
Çalhanoğlu, Hakan 16, 18, 46–7,
168
Cannavaro, Fabio 77, 78, 182,
219, 221
Capello, Fabio 30–31, 42, 68, 72,
157, 182, 221
Carroll, Andy 20
Cassano, Antonio 228, 231
Champions League 30, 48, 61,
87, 112, 135, 185, 186, 203
(2002–3) 151–2

(2006–7) 76–7, 186
(2009–10) 79, 153
(2011–12) 80
(2015–16) 112–13, 203
(2021–22) 17, 18, 20–21, 76,
197, 200–201, 230
ZI's goals in 151–2, 153
Chan, Jackie 24, 159
Chapron, Tony 173–4
Chelsea FC 76, 78–9, 187, 203
Chiellini, Giorgio 4, 52, 219
Chivu, Cristian 213
coaches
as friends 215–17
as opponents 78–82
See also individual coaches' names
commentators 49–50, 81–2,
140–41
communication 134–46
American talk shows
144–6
press 134–44
See also media/press
Community Shield, FA (2016)
155
consultants, business 132, 141,
212
Conte, Antonio 81–2
Coppa Italia 14, 73–6
Córdoba, Iván 69
Costacurta, Billy 169
Covid-19 54–5, 57, 63, 65, 74, 76,
131, 163, 166, 234
Croatia 163
Cruyff, Johan 24

Dacourt, Olivier 227
Dagens Nyheter 138
Dainelli, Dario 153
Dario (physio) 112, 119–20,
　　121, 188, 190, 194, 195–6,
　　199
De Bruyne, Kevin 113, 213–14
De Laurentiis, Aurelio 9–10
Del Piero, Alessandro 230
Den Bosch, FC 29
Denmark (national football
　　team) 26, 213–14
diet 198
discipline 5, 100, 101, 104–6,
　　175–7, 198
Di Vaio, Marco 206
Donnarumma, Gianluigi 16–17,
　　220–22, 224, 228
Dragon Ball 159
dribbling 2, 12, 41–65, 98, 208,
　　214
　　Ajax and 41
　　Barcelona/Guardiola and
　　　43–5
　　Brazilians, ZI studies 41–2
　　Capello on 42
　　flip-flap 41, 42
　　stepover 42
　　ZI's changing game and 42–3
　　ZI's childhood and 41
　　See also freedom

Edmílson, José 151–2
England (national football team)
　　19–23, 25, 84, 149, 219, 222

England, attitudes towards ZI
　　in 19–23, 25, 116–22,
　　141–2, 153, 177
English Football League Cup
　　(EFL) (2017) 155–6
Enrique, Luis 44–5
Eriksen, Christian 46
Escape to Victory (film) 24
Estádio da Luz, 'the Cathedral',
　　Lisbon 152–3
Europa League (2016–17) 119,
　　187–8
European Championship,
　　UEFA
　　(2004) 84
　　(2020) 46, 47, 48, 212–14,
　　218–20, 222
Everton 74

Federcalcio (Italian Football
　　Federation) 180
Ferrari Enzo 128
fines 63, 182–6
Fiorello (Italian TV presenter)
　　58, 62
flip-flap 41, 42
footballs 2, 83–5, 98
freedom
　　burden of being a footballer
　　　47–9
　　cars and 53–4
　　clothing and 52–3
　　Covid and 54–5
　　nature and 51
　　playbook/Guardiola and 43–5

retirement and 49–52
Sanremo Music Festival and
55–65
shirt/club loyalty and 45–7
friendship
AC Milan and 217–18,
220–32
childhood friends of ZI
214–15
coaches and 215–17
Donnarumma 220–24
40th birthday of ZI and
226–32
friend from history to have
dinner with (Muhammad
Ali) 224
isolation of ZI 215
Italian national team and
218–22
Maxwell 213, 215
Mino Raiola *see* Raiola, Mino
money and 214–15
penalties and 222–4
PSG and 217
Red (English bulldog) 224–6
Fu, Freddie 190–96, 207

Gabbiadini, Manolo 155–6
Galbiati, Italo 31
Galliani, Adriano 80, 89, 106,
107–8, 110, 118, 154, 186,
228, 230–31
Gattuso, Gennaro 'Rino' 2, 4,
10, 11, 73, 79, 82, 153–4,
165, 228, 231

Gazidis, Ivan 14–15, 206
Gazzetta dello Sport 29
Giorgio (personal physio) 199
Girondins de Bordeaux, FC 35
goals 147–66
AC Milan–Genoa (2010–11)
153–4
AC Milan–Lazio (2021) 42,
156
Arsenal–Barcelona (2009–10
Champions League) 153
Benfica–Juventus (2005)
152–3, 154
bicycle kick vs England
(international friendly,
2012) 19–23, 25, 84, 149
celebration 147–8, 151
Champions League, ZI's first
goal in 151–2
English Football League Cup
(2017) 155–6
FA Community Shield (2016)
155
family and 160–65
feeling of scoring 147
first 149
happiness and 149, 148, 151,
165–6
importance of 156–7
Kennet Andersson (World
Cup 1994) 149, 150
La Manga (March 2001)
150–51
Lecce–AC Milan (2010–11)
154

goals – *cont'd*
    Marseille–PSG (2012) 154–5
    MLS debut 123–5
    need for 158
    obsession with 157–8
    Parma–Inter (2007–8) 153
    samurai plait and 159–60
    untied boots and 158–9
Göteborg 29
Gravić, Jurka (ZI's mother) 3,
    99–100, 149, 162–3
Guardiola, Pep 11, 29, 43–4, 45,
    69, 79, 153
'Gypsy' (opposition fans label
    ZI) 233, 236, 238

Hammarby Fotboll 27, 92, 98
happiness
    childhood of ZI and 161–2
    children of ZI and 166
    father of ZI and 163–4
    goals and 148, 149, 151, 165–6
    mother of ZI and 162–3
    wife of ZI and 164–5
Hart, Joe 21
Hazard, Thorgan 213–14
Henry, Thierry 33
Hernández, Theo 101, 238
hunting 132–3, 227

Ibrahimović, Helena (ZI's wife)
    7, 9, 107, 145
    energy 165
    extension of ZI's Milan
      contract and 95–7

finances 127, 128–9
first lives with ZI 164–5
first meets ZI 164
football nurtures relationship
    with ZI 87–8
40th birthday of ZI and 2,
    226, 230
furnishing/interior design
    and 3–4, 130
injuries of ZI and 119, 189
media and 135
memorabilia of ZI and 84
Milan apartment of ZI and
    233
New York, first trip to with
    ZI 164
relationship with ZI 3–4,
    5, 88
sons and 85, 93, 95–7, 99, 100,
    101, 127, 160–61, 165
toughness 165
Ibrahimović, Maximilian (ZI's
    son) 1, 89–102
birth 48, 160–61
change to ZI's life with
    arrival of 38–9, 48
discipline and 99–102, 177
fame of ZI and 90, 177
football career and 27, 85,
    90–95, 96, 98, 99, 122,
    148–9, 226
40th birthday of ZI and 231
grandmother and 163
importance of to ZI 4, 38–9,
    89–90, 166

memorabilia and 84
mother and 165
social media and 89–90
solid personality 92
surname choice 92
training 99–102, 122
Ibrahimović, Sanela (ZI's sister)
162
Ibrahimović, Sapko (ZI's
brother) 201–4
Ibrahimović, Šefik
(ZI's father)
discipline and 175–7
football career 163–4
martial arts and 23–4, 159
ZI's adult relationship with
134, 163–4
ZI's childhood and 3, 24,
127–8, 148–9, 159, 162,
175–7
Ibrahimović, Vincent (son)
birth 48, 160–61
change to ZI's life with
arrival of 38–9, 48
discipline and 99–102, 177
fame of ZI and 90, 177
football career and 27, 85,
90–95, 96, 98–9, 122,
148–9, 226
40th birthday of ZI and 231
grandmother and 163
importance of to ZI 4,
38–9, 89–90, 93–4, 166
memorabilia and 84
mother and 127, 165

separation from ZI, reaction
to 48, 93–4, 95, 96–8
social media and 89–90
solid personality 92
surname choice 92
training 99–102, 122
Ibrahimović, Zlatan
adrenaline and see adrenaline
agent see Raiola, Mino
arrogance, accused of 36–8,
116, 141
being yourself, love of 64
bicycle kicks v, 19–23, 24, 25,
29, 31, 40, 84, 98, 149, 209,
230
boats 9, 51, 60, 101, 102, 131,
216, 224
business interests 52, 130, 132,
141, 165, 212
cars 53–4, 115, 128–9, 179
childhood 2–3, 23–6, 40,
62, 66–7, 83–4, 85–6, 90,
98, 99–100, 127–8, 129,
149, 150, 152, 161–2,
175–6, 228
children see Ibrahimović,
Maximilian and
Ibrahimović, Vincent
clothing 52–3
coaches see individual coaches'
names
commentator, TV 140–41
Covid-19 and see Covid–19
crowds, reaction to 5, 54–5
dribbling see dribbling

Ibrahimović, Zlatan – *cont'd*
England, attitudes towards in
19–23, 25, 116–22, 141–2,
153, 177
fame 50–51, 54, 90, 139, 177,
214
father and *see* Ibrahimović,
Šefik
finances 11, 52, 126–9, 130,
132, 141, 212, 214–15
flexibility 23
footballs 83–5
forest land, buys 132–3
40th birthday 226–32, 239
freedom and *see* freedom
friendship and *see* friendship
future 104, 233–40
goals *see* goals
greatest Swedish athletes of
all time and 138–9
heading 24
hunting 132–3, 227
injuries *see* injuries
Italian people, gratitude
towards 59–60
laws and *see* laws
love and 83–102 *see also*
Ibrahimović, Helena;
Ibrahimović, Maximilian
and Ibrahimović,
Vincent
martial arts, love of 23–4, 94,
156, 159, 167
media and *see* media
memorabilia and 84

mother and *see* Gravić,
Jurka
numbers, fascinated by 99
opponents 66–82 *see also*
opponents
passing and *see* passing
penalties and *see* penalties
press and *see* media
private jet travel 127
property 129–32
referees *see* referees
retirement, thoughts of 4,
7–8, 49–52, 95–6, 104, 166,
239
samurai plait 159–60
Sanremo Music Festival 5,
55–65, 76
school 3, 149, 162, 175, 176
second-place finish, refusal to
celebrate 21
selfies and 53, 63, 91
sendings-off 66, 75, 76,
168–9
statue, Malmö 26, 27–8
taking the knee and 238–9
training *see* training
injuries 3, 60, 63, 119–20, 156,
171, 178, 181, 182,
187–207
ZI's cruciate ligament/
Manchester United 7, 72,
119, 187–96
ZI's diet and 198
ZI's left hand 187
ZI's left knee196–7

ZI's personal physio and 199

ZI's recovery time and 198

ZI's style of play and 197–8

ZI's tendons/tendinitis 187, 197, 199–201

Instagram 38, 71–2, 89, 114, 115, 141

Inter Milan 187, 199, 209

    Çalhanoğlu decision to join 46

    Conte and 81–2

    derbies 69–76

    fans 38, 64, 70

    Mancini and 43, 218

    Mourinho and 79

    passing at 213

    Ronaldo and 42

    Scudetto (2020–21) 17, 18

    ZI joins 185–6

    ZI's goals for 153

    ZI's injuries at 187, 234

    ZI's rivalries/opponents at 67–76

Inzaghi, Pippo 71, 158, 210

Italy (national football team) 84, 167–8, 218–20, 222

Jerring Award 138

Jimmy Kimmel Live! 145

Juventus 18, 178, 223

    Capello at 42, 72

    Coppa Italia (2019–20) 14

    fans 64

    Pirlo and 50

referees/Calciopoli match-fixing scandal 180–82, 184–5

ZI joins 59, 164–5

ZI leaves 81

ZI's goals for 31, 42, 152–3, 154

ZI's injuries at 196, 197

ZI's opponents at 66, 67–8, 72, 77–8

Kane, Harry 45

Kardashian, Kim 111–12, 145

Kessié, Franck 158, 223, 224, 237–8

Khelaïfi, Nasser Al- 103, 104, 105, 106, 112–13

Kirovski, Jovan 122

Koeman, Ronald 29, 152–3

LAFC 125

LA Kings 125

LA Lakers 125, 126

La Manga 146, 150–51

Larsson, Henrik 137

Late Late Show with James Corden, The 145–6

Lavezzi, Ezequiel 112, 211, 213, 217

law

    Calciopoli match-fixing scandal 180–82

    family and 175–7

    fines/discipline 182–6

    referees 167–75, 180–82

    traffic regulations 179

    training 177–9

Lazio, SS 42, 69, 156, 158–9,
    171–2, 178, 197, 199, 200
Leão, Rafael 16, 228, 229, 237
Leboeuf, Frank 36–7
Lecce 88–9, 143, 154
Lee, Bruce 24, 159
Leicester City 155
Leiva, Lucas 171–2
Leonardo (Leonardo Araújo)
    105, 108, 109, 110, 112
Le Pen, Marine 37
leukaemia 200–205
Ligue 1. *See* Paris Saint-Germain
    (PSG)
Linde, Peter 28
Lingard, Jesse 155
Liverpool FC 197, 200–201
Lorient, FC 173–4
Los Angeles Galaxy 7, 27, 32–5,
    122–4
    play-offs and, ZI on 33–5
    ZI joins 33, 122–6, 196
    ZI leaves 7–8, 126
    ZI renews contract 125–6
    ZI's debut 123–5
love 83–102
    childhood and 85–6
    children and 89–102
    footballs and 83–5
    love life, ZI's 86–8 *see also*
        Ibrahimović, Helena
    team presidents and 88–9
Lúcio 69, 70
Lukaku, Romelu 63, 72–6, 144
Lyonnais, Olympique 151–2

Maicon 209, 213
Major League Soccer (MLS)
    play-offs 33–5
    quality of 33–5, 122–6
    Rooney in 32
    ZI joins 33, 122–6, 196
    ZI leaves 7–8, 126
    ZI's debut in 123–5
Majstorović, Daniel 227
Malar, Lake 51, 132–3
Maldini, Paolo 10–11, 13, 46, 54,
    60, 75, 219, 220
Malmö, Sweden 26–8, 83, 86,
    87, 97, 99, 129, 132, 163,
    203
Malmö FF 3, 27, 28, 128, 176,
    215, 227
Manchester City 45, 112–13
Manchester United 7, 32, 72, 74,
    114–22, 142, 155–6, 231
    cup wins, ZI's 155–6
    England, attitudes towards
        ZI in and 116–22, 141–2,
        153
    Lukaku and 72, 74
    Manchester, ZI's life in 117
    mindset within club 117–19
    Mourinho and 120–22
    Pogba, ZI chemistry with 213
    power of 156
    Rooney and 31–2, 117, 121
    ZI joins 114–15, 116–17
    ZI leaves 121–3
    ZI's injuries at 7, 119–22,
        187–96

Mancini, Roberto 43, 153, 218

Maradona, Diego 8, 9, 24, 25

Marchegiani, Luca 42

Maresca, Enzo 169

Marseille, Olympique de 154

martial arts 23–4, 94, 156, 159, 167

Martin, Max 227

Massara, Frederic 13

Materazzi, Marco 30, 67–72, 76

Maxwell 108, 115, 116, 132, 213, 215

Mbappé, Kylian 104–6

media/press 134–46
  American talk shows 144–6
  commentators 49–50, 81–2, 140–41
  English 141–2
  female 143–4
  French 142
  Italian 143–4
  personal relationships with 139–40
  press conferences 48, 80, 124–5, 136, 142–3, 211
  Swedish 134–9, 142–3

Messi, Lionel Messi 39, 44, 45

Mete, Guðmundur 215

Mihajlović, Siniša 65, 67, 204–6, 218

Moggi, Luciano 181–2, 183–4, 185, 228, 230

Morgan, Wes 155

Motta, Thiago 108, 113

Mourinho, José 32, 78–9, 82, 114, 120–22, 188, 196, 206, 238

Musahl, Dr Volker 190, 196

Napoli, SSC 2, 8–9, 11, 64

Navarro, David 77

Navas, Keylor 222

Nedvěd, Pavel 115, 185, 210

Nesta, Alessandro 11, 77, 78, 219

New York 131–2, 164

Neymar 39, 45

N'Koulou, Nicolas 154

Nocerino, Antonio 209–10

opponents 66–82
  anger and 66–7
  Ballack 66
  coaches 78–82
  defenders 77–8
  losing control and 66–7
  Lukaku 72–6
  Materazzi 67–72, 76
  Mihajlović 67
  Nesta 78
  Toldo 76–7
  Vieira 77–8

Padel Zenter, Stockholm 132–3

pain
  death and 201–7
  injuries *see* injuries
  tattoos and 201

Paris Saint-Germain (PSG) 35–8, 78–9, 142, 199, 212, 215

Paris Saint-Germain
  (PSG) – *cont'd*
  Donnarumma role at 221–2
  French people/press and
    35–8
  friendships at 211, 215, 217,
    221–2
  Mbappé, ZI advises to leave
    for Real Madrid 104–6
  referees and 35–6, 173–4
  sports director, ZI offers
    himself as 103–6
  Verratti arrives at 211–13
  ZI joins 106–13, 211
  ZI leaves 113–14
  ZI's goals for 154
  ZI's injuries at 187, 199
Parma Calcio 1913 63, 153, 168
passing 208–14
  Chivu and 213
  De Bruyne and 213–14
  friendship/bond with
    teammates and 214
  Maicon and 213
  Maxwell and 213
  Nedvěd and 210
  Nocerino and 209–10
  Pogba and 213–14
  Robinho and 210
  Stanković and 213
  Trezeguet and 210–11
  Verratti and 211–13
  ZI's game and 208–9
  See also friendship
Pastore, Javier 108, 112, 211, 213

Pato, Alexandre 210
Pelé 24, 83, 85
penalties 70, 113, 150, 155, 158,
    169, 174, 175, 222–4, 231,
    237–8
Pescara 211
physios 60, 63, 76, 111, 112, 119,
    120, 121, 155, 179, 188,
    194, 199
Pioli, Stefano 11, 13, 14, 19, 54,
    60, 82, 216, 219, 228, 229,
    234
  children of ZI and 101
  goals and 210
  injuries and 197, 200
  personality 216
  player potential and 17
  red cards and 169, 236
  sacking rumours 13–14
  training and 15
  ZI's relationship with 216
play-offs 33–4
Pochettino, Mauricio 221
Pogba, Paul 99, 120, 213–14,
    228, 231
Porsche 3, 115, 128
Premier League 19, 32, 116–22
press. *See* media/press

Qatar 113
Qatar TV 141

RAI (Italian state television) 55,
    59, 63
Raiola, Mino

AC Milan and 7–10, 186
  Donnarumma and 221
  Inter Milan and 186
  Juventus and 59
  LA Galaxy and 123, 125–6
  Manchester United and
    114–16
  Moggi and 181, 184
  press and 140
  PSG and 103, 104, 106,
    107–8, 109, 110, 113, 221
  ZI first meets 3, 139
  ZI's career trajectory and 3, 5
  ZI's 40th birthday and 227
  ZI's friendship with 3, 214,
    224–5, 227
  ZI's injuries and 189–90, 191,
    193, 194, 195
Rangnick, Ralf 13, 14
Ranieri, Claudio 155
Ranocchia, Andrea 153
Real Madrid 81, 103, 104, 106,
  150
Rebić, Ante 47, 156, 158, 168
Red (English bulldog) 224–6
red cards 66, 75, 76, 168–9
Red Star Belgrade 186
referees v, 4, 76, 167–82, 185,
  235, 236, 237, 238
  attitude towards, ZI changes
    5, 35–6, 66, 167–8, 236
  background of 170–71
  Calciopoli match-fixing
    scandal/Juventus and
    180–82, 185

female 175
  intimidated by ZI 169–70
  Ligue 1 35–6, 173–5
  MLS and 174
  racist insults and 236–8
  red cards and 66, 75, 76,
    168–9
  retired footballers as 170
  Serie A and 168–9, 180–82,
    185, 236, 238
  Video Assistant Referee
    (VAR) 171, 174
Reina, Pepe 172–3
Robinho 210
Roma, AS 60–61, 79, 158, 216,
  234–8
Romagnoli, Alessio 73, 221
Romania (national football
  team) 149, 150
Romário 41
Ronaldinho 99
Ronaldo, Cristiano 45
Ronaldo ('The Phenomenon')
  41, 42, 150, 152
Rooney, Wayne 31–2, 117,
  121
Rydell, Sven 139

Sacchi, Arrigo 29–30
Saelemaekers, Alexis 73, 172,
  173, 216
Saka, Bukayo 219
samurai plait 159–60, 197
Sanremo Music Festival 5,
  55–65, 76

San Siro Stadium, Milan 61, 62, 65, 88, 96, 143, 160, 170, 206, 230, 233
Sarri, Maurizio 82, 171–3
Secco, Alessio 183, 184
Select ball 2, 83–4, 98
selfies 53, 63, 91
Serie A. *See individual teams' names*
Serie B 185, 211, 213
Shawcross, Ryan 22
Shevchenko, Andriy 71, 231
Silva, Thiago 11, 77, 78, 110, 112, 211
Sirigu, Salvatore 112, 132, 213, 228
Slegers, Thijs 139
Southampton FC 155
Southgate, Gareth 222
Stadio Olimpico 60, 234, 238
Stam, Jakob 219
Stanković, Dejan 71, 209, 213
stepover 42
Suárez, Luis 45
Sweden (national football team) 136–7, 239–40
    World Cup *see* World Cup
    ZI bicycle kick vs England (international friendly, 2012) 19–23, 25, 84, 149
    ZI top scorer in history of 139
Swedish Football Association 27, 135–6

Taekwondo 23, 94, 156, 167
taking the knee 238–9
talk shows, American 144–6
Tao Pai Pai 159
Tare, Igli 172
Tătăruşanu, Ciprian 18
tattoos 201
tendinitis 197–201
Terry, John 187
Thuram, Lilian 77, 78, 182, 219, 221
Toldo, Francesco 76–7
Tonali, Sandro 158, 228–9
Topčagić, Nada: 'Jutro je' 62, 227, 228
Torino FC 154
Tottenham Hotspur 82
Totti, Francesco 39, 46
traffic regulations 179
training
    AC Milan 11–13, 15–16, 18–19
    age and 8, 49
    bicycle kicks and 23
    children and 92, 101, 122
    frequency of 48, 49
    injuries and 119, 120, 194, 196
    law of 177–8
    opponents during 68, 78
    winning mentality during 33, 34, 94, 95, 119, 120, 177–8
Trezeguet, David 210–11, 230
Trump, Donald 131–2

Trump SoHo complex,
    Manhattan 131–2

Udinese Calcio 60
UEFA 63, 180
UEFA Cup (1998) 42
UEFA European
    Championship *see* European
    Championship, UEFA
ultras 16–17, 27, 70
United Arab Emirates 113
Unknown (ZI's boat) 9, 51, 60,
    101, 102, 131, 216, 224
UPMC (University of
    Pittsburgh Medical Center)
    190–96

Valencia Club de Fútbol 76–7
van Basten, Marco 29, 30, 31,
    42, 45, 138, 157
van Bommel, Mark 77

Vardy, Jamie 155
Vela, Carlos 125
Verratti, Marco 106, 112, 132,
    211–13, 217, 228
Video Assistant Referee (VAR)
    171, 174, 237
Vieira, Patrick 77–8
Voetbal International 139

Welbeck, Danny 22
West, Kanye 111–12
Woodward, Ed 114–15
World Cup
    (1994) 138, 149, 150
    (2018) 141
    (2022) 239–40

Zambrotta, Gianluca 227,
    231
Zebina, Jonathan 182–3
Zidane, Zinedine 25, 152

I AM ZLATAN IBRAHIMOVIĆ
ZLATAN IBRAHIMOVIĆ

'Why be a Fiat when you can be a Ferrari?'

Welcome to planet Zlatan. This is the story of how a Swedish immigrant rose from poverty to become a football genius.

In his own inimitable style, Zlatan recalls every struggle, every goal and every training ground bust-up on his journey to dominate the world's top clubs, including Barcelona, PSG and Manchester United.

Full of wicked one-liners and amazing stories, Zlatan lifts the lid on some of the biggest names in football, including Guardiola, Messi and José Mourinho.

Moving, funny and totally frank, *I am Zlatan Ibrahimović* is unlike any autobiography you have ever read.

'Wonderful – nothing less than a revelation. Ibrahimović is the definitive modern sporting icon'

Matthew Syed

'The best sportsman's memoir since Andre Agassi . . . not just a bad boy's romp but the rise of a boy from the ghetto to the top of his profession and captain of his country. He is candid, funny and, yes, wonderfully nuts'

The Times

'There's never a dull moment on planet Zlatan. This is a snarling, fizzing, unrepentant firecracker of a book; if footballers' memoirs bore you, make an exception for this one'

Independent